Hidden Meanings

Truth and Secret
in Haiti's Creole Proverbs

Wally R. Turnbull

D1273328

Hidden Meanings

Truth and Secret
in Haiti's Creole Proverbs

A collection of over 1300
Haitian Creole proverbs featuring
English translations
and interpretations

Wally R. Turnbull

Torchflame Books

Durham, NC

This book is dedicated to my father, Wallace, who has spent his life bringing Truth to Hidden Meanings.

CONTENTS

PREFACE

Hidden Meanings: Truth and Secret in Haiti's Creole Proverbs is a collection of the colorful proverbs that characterize this country and its people. Whenever possible, literal rather than common translations are provided that the reader may hear the language as well as the proverbs. We have also included explanations of the proverbs' meanings. In many cases, the uses and interpretations of a proverb are as deep and varied as those who speak it, and we have done our best to offer the most common and relevant interpretations. When a proverb has more than one possible use and meaning both interpretations are sometimes but not always given. In some instances, alternate interpretations are clear from the translation. In other cases, they may be seldom used.

Translating a Creole proverb into English requires a fluency of not only both languages, but also of culture, an idiom more difficult to learn than any offered in a grammar book.

Wally Turnbull, born to missionary parents and raised in the mountains of Haiti, has learned to communicate with his neighbors on a level few attain, speaking their language of simple images and hidden meanings. For many years, it has been his dream to collect the beloved sayings and share them with the outside world. This book is the result of three decades of collection, translation, and interpretation, but as the Haitian people will tell you, *"it takes patience to see the navel of the ant."*

Featuring over 1300 entries, this is, to date, the most varied, complete, and accurate collection of Haitian proverbs, though one can never know all the wisdom of this people, for it grows with each new obstacle and generation born.

We hope that the people of Haiti as well as foreigners who love Haiti will enjoy and learn from *Hidden Meanings* as it opens a new window to a rich and colorful culture, learning that understanding comes not from a book or classroom, but rather from a patient perspective on life and those who surround us.

Elizabeth J. Turnbull

Cautions and Council

Si tèt ou pa travay, pye ou va travay.
If your head doesn't work, your feet will work.

Tout sa ou pa konnen pi gran pase ou.
All that you do not know is greater than you.

Dèyè mòn gen mòn.
Behind mountains there are mountains.
There's a hidden meaning to what is being said.

Pa kite yè gaspiye jodi a.
Don't let yesterday waste today.
Don't waste time reliving the past.

Se pa tout bagay ki aprann lekòl.
Not everything is learned at school.
Some things are mysteries. Some lessons in life must be learned from experience.

Si ou pa t'ap fikse syèl la, ou pa ta wè tan kouvè.
If you were not staring at the sky you would not have seen that it is cloudy.
Don't look for trouble.

Pa mete pye nan tout soulye.
Don't put your foot in every shoe.
Don't meddle with things that don't concern you.

Pa koke makout ou pi wo pase men ou.
Don't hang your bag higher than your hand.
Don't get into a situation that surpasses your ability.

Vant grangou fè lapriyè kout.
A hungry belly makes a short prayer.
Let's get to it. Cut to the chase. When you are in a hurry you take shortcuts.

Avan ou monte bwa, gade si ou ka desann li.
Before you climb a tree, look to see if you can climb down.
Make sure you know what you're getting into.

Atansyon pa kapon.
Careful isn't cowardly.
Being cautious does not make you a coward.

Jan chache, Jan twouve, Jan anbarase.
John seeks, John finds, John is in an awkward position.
Be careful about what you seek or where you meddle.

Yo pa ranmase dlo ki tonbe.
Spilled water is not picked up.
Don't cry over an incident that is in the past.

Tout koukouy klere pou je pa yo.
Every firefly shines for its own eyes.
Every person thinks he or she is perfect. Each person should take care of himself.

Pwason gen konfyans nan dlo e se dlo ki kwit li.
A fish trusts water, but it is water that cooks it.
Don't take anything for granted. Your home environment can prove to be the most dangerous.

Begeyè pèdi.
He who stammers looses.
Hurry up and make up your mind.

W'ap kabicha pou manje manje moun chich.
You are falling asleep waiting to eat a stingy person's food.
You are wasting your time.

De kòk kalite pa rete nan menm baskou.
Two good roosters don't stay in the same yard.
Each situation needs only one leader.

Kal pwason pa lajan.
A fish scale isn't money.
Not everything that looks pretty has value.

Anbisyon touye rat.
Ambition kills the rat.
The overly ambitious get into trouble.

Tout sa ou pa konnen pi gran pase w'.
All that you do not know is greater than you.
Knowledge is power. One fears the unknown.

Bon boy pa monte.
The good dumpling does not float.
Good things are not easy. Good people are hard to find.

Pwason nan lanmè pa tande dlo k'ap bouyi pou yo.
The fish in the sea don't hear water boiling for them.
When things are going well you don't think about danger.

Si w' te plante manyòk ou pa ka fouye patat.
If you planted cassava you can't harvest sweet potatoes.
Consequences. You reap what you sow.

Pasyans bèl, lavi long.
Patience is beautiful, life is long.
A patient person is happier.

Zanmòrèt pa berejèn.
The turkeyberry is not eggplant. (Turkeyberry leaves look like eggplant but the fruit is inedible.)
Appearances can be deceiving.

Pwason pa byen ak nas.
The fish is not friendly with the net.
Stay away from those who want to take advantage of you.

Lè w' mouri ou pa konnen, lè w' konnen ou mouri.
When you die, you don't know; when you know, you die.
Knowledge comes at the end of life.

Se lè bèf nan savann wè bouche li sonje voye je pou li.
It is when the cow in the pasture sees the butcher that she remembers to look out for him.
When things are going too well you forget about danger.

Pa gen zèl pa jwe ak zwazo.
No wings don't play with birds.
Don't go beyond your competency.

Pye pa gen rasin.
A foot has no root.
One can always fall. One can always leave.

Lè y'ap plimen poul kodenn pa ri.
When the chicken is being plucked, the turkey doesn't laugh.
Don't laugh at others' misfortune, for it could happen to you, too.

Yon sèl dwèt pa manje kalalou.
One finger doesn't eat okra.
People should cooperate in a sticky situation.

Ou pa ka fè san soti nan wòch.
You can't draw blood from a stone.
You can't have what does not exist.

Bèf plizyè mèt mouri grangou.
A cow of many masters dies of hunger.
When no one is assigned responsibility, the job doesn't get done.

Ou konn kouri men ou pa konn kache.
You know how to run, but you don't know how to hide.
You can run, but you can't hide. You will be found.

Fòk ou dòmi ak Jan pou konnen si l' wonfle.
You must sleep with John to know if he snores.
Only first hand knowledge can be sure of the truth.

Byen prese pa rive.
In a big hurry doesn't arrive.
Hurrying too much keeps you from achieving your goal.

Avan tiraj tout nimewo bèl.
Before the drawing all numbers look good.
False hope. All things seem equal but that is not the case.

Gwo vant pa lajan.
A big stomach isn't money.
Appearances can be deceiving.

Gwo vant pa gwosès.
A big stomach isn't pregnancy.
Don't jump to conclusions.

Gwo tèt pa lespri.
A large head isn't intelligence.
Don't mistake self-assurance for intelligence.

Zafè nèg pa janm piti.
A man's business is never small.
Never belittle another person's plans. What a person wants to do is important to him.

Makak pa janm twò vye pou l' voye wòch.
A monkey is never too old to throw rocks.
One person is never too old to hurt another.

Konplo pi fò pase wanga.
A plot is stronger than a witchdoctor's fetish.
A plan is better than magic.

Sèvis ranvwaye ranje moun touni.
A postponed ceremony accomodates the naked person.
Putting off helps those who are not prepared.

Tout sa ki klere pa lò.
All that shines isn't gold.
Looks can be deceiving.

Mwen pa renmen pantouf apre pwomnad.
I don't like slippers after a walk.
You have made me run around and waste time, now don't try to make me happy with soft words.

Tout liann nan bwa se pèlen.
Every vine in the woods is a trap.
Be careful of dangerous situations.

Apre kase mayi, n'a konte boujon.
After harvesting the corn, we'll count the sprouts.
Don't count on results prematurely.

Yon sèl papiyon pa fè lasenjan.
A single butterfly doesn't make Saint John's holiday.
A single sign might not mean anything. Get more facts.

Lougawou pa manje lougawou parèy li.
A werewolf doesn't eat other werewolves.
Just because they get along doesn't mean that you can trust either one of them.

Tout bèt jennen mòde.
All cornered animals bite.
There are certain situations in which any person will react.

Lanmò toujou gen koz.
Death always has a reason.
Everything has a reason for it. There is always an explanation.

Bat chen an, tann mèt li.
Beat the dog; wait for its master.
Don't abuse another person's property. The weak may well have powerful protectors.

Pasyans bèl, lavi long.
Patience is beautiful, life is long.

Wè jodi a men sonje demen.
See today, but remember tomorrow.

Zwazo pose sou tout branch.
Birds land on all branches.
Your turn will come.

Avan chen manje zo, li mezire machwè l'.
Before a dog eats a bone, he sizes his jaw.
Don't take on more than you can handle.

Mande vagabon sa l' manje, pa mande l' sa l' konnen.
Ask the vagabond what he eats; don't ask him what he knows.
Don't ask the dishonest about their deeds.

Anvan ou ri moun bwete, gade jan ou mache.
Before you laugh at a lame man, watch how you walk.
Don't criticize another until you have fixed your own faults.

Pito ou solda nan paradi ou pa chèf nan lanfè.
Better to be a soldier in paradise than a chief in hell.
Happiness is better than power.

Pito ou mache sou "pinga" pou ou pa pile "si m' te konnen".
Better to walk on "don't" than to step in "if I'd only known."
Caution now prevents regret later.

Pa kontrarye danje si twou poko fouye pou antere malè.
Don't annoy danger if misfortune's grave is not yet dug.
If you look for trouble, you might find it.

Berejèn pa janm pran koulè.
Eggplant never changes color.
Some things never change.

Kenbe kabrit nwa anvan l' fè nwa.
Catch a black goat before it gets dark.
Act before it is too late.

Byen pre pa lakay.
Close isn't home.
Being close doesn't count.

Bèf ak ke pa janbe dife.
Cows with tails don't cross fires.
Those with a secret past should not get in trouble.

Madichon pa pè nan nwit.
Curses don't fear the night.
Bad things happen during the night.

Pinga miyò pase malè.
Don't is better than misfortune.
Avoid trouble.

Pa antre nan batay san baton.
Don't go to battle without a club.
Be prepared.

Pa touye tèt ou pou piman pou lè pwav bon mache pou ou pa jwi li.
Don't kill yourself for hot peppers, lest when black pepper is cheap, you can't enjoy it.
It is better to wait for what you really want.

Pa kite bourik pou bat makout.
Don't miss the donkey and beat the saddlebag.
Don't blame the wrong one.

Pa kite moun koupe zèb anba pye ou.
Don't let people cut the grass under your feet.
Don't let people take advantage of you.

Pa pran chans; pa pèdi chans.
Don't take risk; don't loose luck.
It is better to be safe than sorry.

Kabrit bwè, mouton sou.
Goats drink, sheep get drunk.
Avoid that lifestyle. You are better than that. It will hurt you more.

Pa manyen nèg ki benyen nan gwo dlo.
Don't touch a man who bathes in deep water.
Be careful with those who have high connections.

Pousyè pa leve san van.
Dust doesn't rise without wind.
Trouble doesn't start without instigation.

Pi bonè se gran maten.
The earliest is dawn.
An early start is the best.

Zanno kase nan sak pa pèdi.
Earrings that break in a sack are not lost.
One is safe where one belongs.

Pito ou lèd, men ou vivan.
Better you're ugly, but living.
Count your blessings.

Ranje kabann ou anvan dòmi nan je ou.
Make your bed before you are sleepy.
Plan ahead.

Je pa dan; dwèt pa kòn.
Eyes aren't teeth; fingers aren't horns.
Don't take on more than you can handle. Know your limits.

Nonm sa a se mouch pa poze.
Even flies don't land on that man.
Stay away from him.

Bon pa dire.
Good doesn't last.
The best are selected first. A good worker is overworked.

Byen lwen pa nan Ginen.
Far away isn't in Guinea.
Far away isn't history. It's not over yet. It isn't far enough.

Pou yon tab byen kanpe fòk li gen kat pye menm longè.
For a table to stand well, it must have all four legs the same length.
To work well together, people should be equal.

Demi kwit sove, konsonmen pèdi.
Half-cooked saved, broth lost.
It's too late for some but not for others.

Prese kon ou prese, twò prese pa fè jou louvri.
Hurry as you may, too much hurrying doesn't make the sun come up.
Take it easy. One step at a time.

Si koukouy pa t' klere nan nuit, yo pa ta kenbe l'.
If the firefly didn't glow at night, they wouldn't catch it.
Showing off gives the crook away.

Sa ki mare Bouki, li ki pou lage l'.
He who ties Bouki is the one to loosen him.
Don't mess with what you don't know.

Lavi se tè glise.
Life is a slippery land.
Life is unpredictable.

Kenbe chen ou, m'a kenbe baton m'.
Hold back your dog and I'll hold back my stick.
Don't bother me and I won't bother you. The situation is a stand-off.

Nan bay kout men, ou jwen kout pye.
In giving a hand, you receive a foot (kick).
Ingratitude. Criticism of the way help is offered.

Mwen mete l' devan pou m' wè mach li.
I put him in front so that I might see his walk.
I'm keeping my eye on him.

M' pa'p rele chen "Papa" pou zo.
I won't call a dog "Father" for a bone.
It is not worth it. There are limits.

Si kafou pa bay, simityè pa jwenn.
If the crossroad doesn't provide, the cemetery doesn't
receive.
Only things that are meant to be will happen.

M'ap pote ou sou do m'; ou pa ka di ou pile teta.
I'm carrying you (across the river) on my back; you can't tell
me you stepped on a tadpole.
*I was there. I know better. Don't complain about the help you're
receiving.*

M' pa'p soti nan zòrey pou m' al nan talon.
I'm not going to leave the ear to go on the heel.
I already have access to someone more important.

Si makak di ou l'ap ba ou yon kout wòch, konnen wòch
li nan men l'.
If the monkey tells you he's going to hit you with a rock,
know that the rock is in his hand.
Be prepared when threatened.

Si m'ap fè ou labab, pa pase men ou, w'a blese.
If I'm shaving you, don't wipe your face or you'll get cut.
I'm taking care of that for you. Stay out of it.

Se je ki gad kò.
Your eyes are your bodyguards.
Being on the look out keeps one safe.

Si se pa t' fèy la, mwen ta touye zwazo a.
If it were not for the leaf, I would kill the bird.
You are spared because of your surroundings.

Si ou jwe ak dife, dife va boule ou.
If you play with fire, fire will burn you.
If you do dangerous things you will get hurt.

Si ou manje bouji, fòk ou poupou mèch.
If you eat a candle, you must pass a wick.
You must pay the consequences of your actions.

Si ou prese twòp, ou p'ap vanse.
If you hurry too much, you won't advance.
Take it easy. One step at a time.

Si ou gade sa poul manje, ou p'ap manje poul.
If you look at what the chicken eats, you won't eat the chicken.
Some things are better left unknown.

Apa se vini w'ap vini? Wa wè.
Is it not coming that you're coming? You'll see.
You are young. You will learn.

Si ou vle wè plezi vye tonton, tòde ke l'.
If you want to see the old man's foolishness, twist his tail.
Put him on the spot and watch him squirm.

Si ou renmen gren andan, ou dwe renmen po a tou.
If you like the nut, you ought to like the shell.
Don't complain about working for something you want.

Pi ta, pi tris.
Later, sadder.
Later it will be too late and you will be sorry.

Devan pòt gen parapòt.
In front of doors are storm doors.
Take extra precautions. Be cautious.

Se mèt kò ki veye kò.
The master of the body watches the body.
Don't leave personal business to others.

Nan twòp piwèt, lougawou kite jou bare l'.
In too much dancing, the werewolf lets day break.
Criminals get caught by bragging and showing off.

Se samdi ki konn si dimanch ap bèl.
It is Saturday that knows if Sunday will be nice.
Don't plan too far ahead.

Li pa janm twò ta pou chen mèg anraje.
It's never too late for the lean dog to go mad.
An abused person may become angry at any moment.

Bo nan bouch, men pè dan.
Kiss on the mouth, but fear the teeth.
Enjoy a situation or person, but be cautious.

Se nan jwèt yo batize jwif.
It's only in jest that they baptize Jews.
He is only pretending.

Se pa bon pou yon moun konnen twòp.
It's not good for a person to know too much.
Knowing too much brings trouble.

Malè pa gen klaksonn.
Misfortune doesn't honk a horn.
Misfortune doesn't give warning.

Fè tan kite tan.
Leave time to time.
Don't waste time reliving the past.

Se lavey ki di ou ki jan fèt la pral ye.
It's the eve that tells you how the party will be.
You never know until the last minute how things will turn out.

Se dlo kò a ki benyen kò a.
It's the water of the body that bathes the body.
Accept what is appropriate.

Pa janm mete chat veye bè.
Never put a cat to watch over the butter.
Don't ask a person to watch over something he may want.

Ri moun kout, men pa ri moun touni.
Laugh at short people, but don't laugh at naked people.
That could be you. You may not be short but everyone can be naked.

Se kan ou pran ou konnen.
It's when you are caught that you know.
Hindsight has perfect vision.

Fin konnen mouri sòt.
Know-it-all dies stupid.
Don't be too sure of yourself, or you will get in trouble.

Prete pa bay.
Lending is not giving.
Return what you borrow.

Chita tande, mache wè.
Sit and hear, walk and see.
Listen to advice but experience for yourself.

Dlo lacho blan, men se pa lèt li ye.
Whitewash is white, but it's not milk.
Looks can be deceiving.

Chache lavi detwi lavi.
Looking for life destroys life.
In searching for an exciting life, one will destroy what life one has.

Mesire anvan ou koupe.
Measure before you cut.
Think before you act.

Se pa tout lè Magrit ale nan mache pou l' pote bèl siwo.
It is not every time that Magrit goes to market that she brings back honey.
Don't expect the best every day.

Lajan fè timoun radi.
Money makes children rascals.
It's not good to have too much too soon.

Pòtoprens vann men li pa bay papye.
Port-au-Prince sells, but it doesn't give a receipt.
Beware of fast talking city slickers.

Lajan pa janm al kay gangan pou l' tounen.
Money never goes to the witchdoctor's house to return.
Whether it works or not, you won't get your money back.

Makòmè Krikèt, si m' pa di ou, ki jan pou ou fè konnen?
Sister Cricket, if I didn't tell you, how could you know?
Don't talk about what you don't know.

Wè sa m' fè; pa fè sa m' fè.
See what I do; don't do what I do.
Do as I say, not as I do. Don't follow my example.

Pa janm pale lougawou mal devan moun.
Never speak bad about a werewolf in front of others.
Evil is disguised in those around you. People will gossip.

Ranmase pyè tonè pa di kont, men se mete l' atè a ki di kont.
Picking up a lightning stone doesn't mean much; it's putting it down that means something.
It's easy to get involved, but not so easy to get out.

Jwe ak dife, dife ka boule ou.
Play with fire, fire can burn you.
Don't do dangerous things or you may get hurt.

Jwèt se jwèt, kròchèt pa ladann.
Playing is playing but there's no tripping.
Teasing must have its limits.

Kouri pou lapli; tonbe nan gran rivyè.
Run from the rain to fall in the river.
To flee from one disaster to a bigger one.

Swen djondjon pou lago.
Protect mushrooms from a game of tag.
Protect the fragile from the rowdy.

Rete trankil se remèd kò.
Staying still is the body's medicine.
Rest makes one well.

Wè pa wè, lantèman pou katrè.
Seen or not, the burial is at four o'clock.
Whether or not it's expected, death comes when it's time. (Four o'clock is the end of the work day.)

File kouto, men veye dwèt ou.
Sharpen your knife, but watch your fingers.
Get ready but be careful.

Fizi tire; nanpwen aranjman.
Shots are fired; there is no more negotiating.
It is too late to compromise. Once a fight begins, talking stops.

Byen chita pa di byen monte.
Sitting (on a horse) well doesn't mean riding well.
Looks don't guarantee performance.

Wè jodi a men sonje demen.
See today, but remember tomorrow.
Live in the present, but plan for the future.

Di "Bonjou, Papa dyab", l'ap manje ou. Di "Bonjou dyab", l'ap manje ou. Di "Bonjou, dyab!"
Say "Good morning Father Devil," he'll devour you. Say "Good morning, Devil," he'll devour you. So, say "Good morning, Devil."
Don't flatter the wicked.

Lafimen pa janm leve san dife.
Smoke never rises without fire.
The signs of trouble don't appear without due cause.

Rete twò lontan nan mache fè ou fè dèt.
Staying too long in the market puts you in debt.
It's time to go home.

Bat bourik la, men manyen chaj li.
Whip the donkey, but rearrange its load.
Punish but understand the cause of the problem. Be merciful. Don't overdo it.

Sa ki rive koukouloukou a ka rive kakalanga tou.
What happens to the cock-a-doodle-do, can happen to the gobble-gobble.
Be careful. What happens to another can happen to you.

Chat mande swe; ou mete chen dèyè l'.
When the cat asks to sweat, you sick the dog on it.
If you want to do it the hard way, that can be arranged.

Sa ki nan vant se li ki pa ou.
What's in your belly is what's yours.
Don't count on something until you have it in hand.

Timoun radi, se nan simityè bab yo pouse.
Naughty children's beards grow in the grave.
Misbehaved children die young.

Kout baton twò fò anpeche chen rete.
Too much beating prevents the dog from stopping.
Overly harsh punishment will only make things worse.

Je pete pa rete gade.
The blind don't stay to gawk.
That's none of your business. There is nothing you can do.

Kòk pa janm mache kite zepon l'.
The cock never leaves his spurs behind.
If you are a leader you must always be prepared for trouble.

Kote y'ap plimen kodenn poul pa ri.
When the turkey is getting plucked, the chicken doesn't laugh.
You must not laugh at others' misfortune, for it could hit you, too.

Mò pa jije.
The dead aren't judged.
It's too late for that, forget it.

Chen gen kat pat; se yon sèl chemen li fè.
The dog has four paws, but it only takes one path.
One thing at a time.

Avèg di l'ap ba ou kout wòch; si l' pa nan men l' li anba pye l'.
When a blind man tells you he is going to hit you with a stone, if it's not in his hand, it's under his foot.
When a threat is given, be prepared even if it seems safe.

Ti poul grate grate; li jwen zo grangrann li.
The chick scratches and scratches; it finds the bones of its great-grandmother.
Be careful of digging into the past.

Jou va; jou vyen.
The day goes; the day comes.
What goes around comes around.

Dyab pa janm bay pou granmesi.
The Devil never gives for nothing. (never gives for thanks.)
Dealings with the wicked carry a price.

Chen ou fè byen, kou li anraje, se ou li mòde.
The dog you are kind to will choose you to bite when it goes mad.
People often hurt those who are the closest to them.

Makak sou pa dòmi devan pòt kay chen.
The drunken monkey doesn't sleep in front of the dog's door.
You have been drinking, be careful. Watch what you do.

Chen cho pran kou.
The eager dog gets the beating.
Don't rush into things.

Ze ki kale twò bonè, ti poul la p'ap viv.
When the egg is hatched early, the chick doesn't live.
Timing is everything. Don't rush.

Malè je wè pa kite l' rive.
The eyes that see misfortune don't let it arrive.
Take heed of warnings.

Jou yon fèy tonbe nan dlo, se pa jou a li pouri.
The day a leaf falls into water is not the day it rots.
It's not over. Down but not out.

Bonbon ou renmen se li ki fini ak kòb ou.
The candy you like is the one that finishes your money.
Bad habits are expensive. Too much of a good thing.

Pwason sot nan dlo, li di ou kayiman malad; kwè li.
The fish jumps from the water and tells you that the
Cayman is sick; believe it.
Take extra heed of special warnings.

Manje ou renmen, se li ki gonfle ou.
The food you enjoy is the one that gives you gas.
What you want may not be good for you.

Chay ou pare pou bèlmè ou, se manman ou ki va pote l'.
The load you prepare for your mother-in-law is the one your
mother will carry.
What you plot for others may come back to hurt you.

Kabrit gade je mèt kay avan l' antre.
The goat looks the master in the eye before he enters.
Learn to understand a person's mood before approaching him.

Malfini pou grann, poul pou grann.
The hawk is Grandma's; the chicken is Grandma's.
*Good and bad children from the same family. Grandparents
love all of their grandchildren.*

Poul ki bat kò l' kraze ze l'.
The hen that thrashes around breaks her eggs.
Take it easy. You'll hurt yourself.

Mamzèl pa pitimi san gadò.
The young lady isn't millet without a guardian.
She has people watching out for her.

Malfini manke ou, li pa bliye ou.
The hawk missed you, but he didn't forget you.
Danger doesn't leave forever.

Ti kòk ki louvri twò bonè pèdi je l'.
The little rooster that spreads too early loses his eyes.
You are too young. You are not ready.

Moun ki mache nan nwit se li ki kontre ak dyab.
The one who walks around at night is the one who meets up with the Devil.
Don't go where you don't belong.

Bonbòn toutouni pa janm al nan priyè wòch galèt.
The naked glass jug does not go to a prayer meeting of the river stones.
One does not put oneself in a vulnerable situation.

Lè timoun fonte mande gonbo cho; ou ba li l' nan pla men l'.
When a pushy child asks for hot okra, give it to him in the palm of his hand.
Teach him a lesson. The naughty ask for trouble and get it.

Fèy palmis pa danse san van.
Palm branches don't dance without wind.
Every effect has a cause. There is a reason for that.

Larivyè avèti pa touye kokobe.
The river forewarned doesn't kill the handicapped.
With a fair warning there should be no excuse.

Mèt kabrit mande kabrit; ou pa ka di li plenn.
The owner of the goat asks for the goat; you can't say she is pregnant.
Don't make excuses to keep what doesn't belong to you.

Lane pase toujou pi bon.
Last year is always better.
The "good old days" always seem better.

Pastè ap danse, l'ap veye nan makout li.
The preacher is dancing; he's looking in his bag.
He's after your money.

Koulèv ki bezwen gwo rete nan twou l'.
The snake that wants to grow stays in its hole.
Those who want to live long stay out of harm's way.

Kochon ki manje kòd, demen maten nan lari ou jwenn li.
The pig that chews his rope will wind up in the street in the morning.
Those with bad habits always end up on the street.

Kote ou frape pye ou se la ou dwe kite l' senyen.
Where you stub your foot is where you should let it bleed.
Don't bother others with your troubles.

Piti piti plen kay.
Little by little the house is filled.
Bit by bit things (also children) add up to be a lot.

Batiman vapè ranni men li pa bèf pou sa.
The steamship bellows, but that doesn't make it a cow.
Don't jump to conclusions.

Moun ki kenbe kiyè bwa se li ki konnen si li cho.
The person who holds the wooden spoon
is the one who knows if it's hot.

Pye bwa ki wo di li wè lwen,
gren pwomennen di li wè pase l'.
The tall tree says it sees far,
the wandering seed says it sees more.

Pye bwa ki wo di li wè lwen. Gren pwomennen wè pase l'.
The tall tree says it sees far. The wandering seed sees more.
Traveling opens one's eyes.

Moun ki mete sèl nan solèy, se li ki veye lapli.
The person who put the salt to dry in the sun is the one who
watches for rain.
Those with something to lose watch for danger.

Rat konnen sa l' fè; li mache nan nwit.
The rat knows what it's doing; it walks at night.
Evil finds safety in the cover of night.

Kòd kenbe pou ou; li pa gade pou ou.
The rope holds for you; it doesn't watch for you.
Let others help you but keep your eyes open as well.

Kochon ki manje kòd se nan gran chemen ou jwen li.
The pig that eats his cord is found on the main road.
People with bad habits seek the fast life.

Tig vye men zong li pa janm vye.
The tiger is old but its claws are never old.
One is never too old to fight back.

Lè bwapini nan men ou; lougawou pè pwoche.
When a thorny club is in your hand; the werewolf is afraid
to approach.
Being prepared keeps one safe.

Ti bwa ou pa wè, se li ki pete je ou.
The twig you don't see is the one that puts out your eye.
Be cautious.

Dlo ou pa pè, se li ki pote w' ale.
The water you don't fear is the one that washes you away.
Over confidence brings about one's end.

Twò prese fè ou bo sou nen.
Too hurried makes you kiss on the nose.
In a hurry, one will miss one's mark.

Jan ou ranje kabann ou se jan ou dòmi.
The way you make your bed is the way you sleep.
Prepare and enjoy or suffer the consequences.

Jan ou marye se pa konsa ou divòse.
The way you marry is not the way you divorce.
Each situation has its own procedure to follow. People behave differently in different circumstances.

Moun ki kenbe kiyè bwa se li ki konnen si li cho.
The person who holds the wooden spoon is the one who knows if it's hot (the food).
Don't question first hand knowledge.

Yo pa ranje tòl kay nan lapli.
House roofs are not repaired in the rain.
Plan ahead.

Van woule pilon; ale wè pou kalbas.
The wind roles the mortar, not to mention the gourd.
A situation which is difficult for important people is impossible for others.

Zonbi gade je mèt kay, anvan l' di, "lonè".
The zombie watches the eyes of the master of the house before he says, "honor."
Wait until the moment is right before making your move. Pay attention to boss' mood before making a request.

Twòp pwofi kreve pòch.
Too much profit splits your pockets.
Too much of a good thing.

Evite miyò pase padon.
Avoiding is better than forgiveness.
It is better to stay out of trouble than to beg forgiveness.

Nanpwen cho ki pa vin frèt.
There's no heat that doesn't cool down.
No situation is permanent.

Yo pa janm chatre chen de fwa.
They never castrate a dog twice.
There's nothing more one can do.

Nèg sa a se yon kat make.
This guy is a marked card.
We know what kind of person he is.

Tan ale; li pa tounen.
Time goes, it doesn't return.
One can never return to the past.

Twò prese pa rive.
Too hurried doesn't arrive.
Don't rush.

Twò byen nwi kò.
Too well off bothers the body.
Too much of a good thing can cause you to get sick.

Kanson kreve pa di razè pou sa.
Torn pants don't mean broke.
Don't jump to conclusions.

Mache chemen ou dwat pou ou pa pile "si m' te konnen".
Walk a straight road so you don't step on "if I had known."
Stay out of trouble.

Veye zo ou pou ou pa pile "si m' te konnen".
Watch your bones so that you don't step on "if only I had known."
Think before you act.

Sa ki atè se pou chen.
What is on the ground is for the dog.
Don't stoop to their level. That is below you.

Veye zo ou.
Watch your bones.
Be careful.

De kou nan dèyè bourik la; de kou nan sak pay la.
Two blows on the donkey's hind end; two on the straw saddle bag.
Don't be overly harsh.

Sa zòtolan di sou bwa, se pa sa l' di lè l' anba pèlen.
What the partridge says on the branch is not what it says when it's in a trap.
The tune of one's words changes depending on circumstances.

Sa ou fè se li ou wè.
What you do is what you see.
You reap what you sow.

Sa ou pa vle touche ak pye ou, ou manyen l' ak men ou.
What you don't want to touch with your foot, you handle with your hands.
Trying to avoid the inevitable will only make matters worse.

Sa ou santi a se nan dife l'ap boukannen.
What you smell is roasting in the fire.
It looks good but you don't know the whole story.

Lè yon chòdyè cho, ou pa desann li ak men.
When a kettle is hot, you don't take it off the fire with your hands.
Don't touch a person when he is angry. Be careful with dangerous situations.

Sa ou plante se sa ou rekòlte.
What you plant is what you harvest.
You reap the consequences of your actions.

Sa w'ap chache anlè, ou jwen li atè.
What you're looking for up high, you find on the ground.
Things lie where you least expect them. The fall of an important person.

Lè labouyi cho, ou manje l' a rebò.
When the pudding is hot, you eat it from the edge.
Go slowly with an angry person.

Se pa lè yon moun ap neye pou ou montre l' naje.
When a person is drowning is not the time to teach him how to swim.
Help now, lecture later.

Sa ou pa wè nan santan, ou wè li nan yon jou.
What you don't see in a hundred years you see in one day.
Unusual but not impossible.

Lè yon bann mouch ap vole, ou pa konn ni mal ni femèl.
In a swarm of flies, you don't know male from female.
In a crowd, one cannot distinguish the harmless from the dangerous.

Lè kè ti poul kontan, konnen malfini pa lwen.
When the chick is happy, know that the hawk is not far.
When a young girl is happy know that she has a suitor.

Avek pasyans w'a wè lonbrit foumi.
With patience you will see the navel of an ant.
It takes patience to notice the small details.

Lè pye bwa jwe ak van, li pèdi fèy li.
When the tree plays with the wind, it loses its leaves.
Mind your own business. Don't go where you don't belong.

Kan dife mouri, timoun jwe nan sann li.
When the fire dies, the children play in its ashes.
When the danger has passed, one feels free to frolic again.

Lè kribich bezwen grandi, se nan twou wòch li rete.
When the crayfish wants to grow, it stays in a hole.
Avoid confrontation.

Kou rat vle mouri, li pran lari.
When the rat wants to die, he takes to the street.
It is safer not to be too visible. Don't flaunt.

Lè dlo ap desann, ou pa foure pye ou.
When the river is raging, you don't stick your foot in it.
There is no such thing as a little danger.

Ou bat tanbou epi ou danse ankò.
You beat the drum and then you dance again.
You set your own pace.

Se pa ak rara yo kenbe zwazo.
You don't catch birds with a carnival band.
You will scare away a person you are trying to convince if you talk too much.

Lè ou pral lwen, ou bay bourik ou dlo.
When you're going far, you give your donkey water.
Plan ahead.

Lè ou gade nan mont ou, wa wè li trèzè.
When you look at your watch, you will see that it's thirteen o'clock.
It's too late.

Lè lougawou frekante ou, atansyon pitit ou.
When the werewolf visits you, watch your children.
If you associate with criminals, those you love may get hurt.

Lè ou an devenn, lèt kaye kase tèt ou.
When you are in bad luck, clabbered milk can break your head.
When you are having bad luck, every little thing seems to go wrong.

Lè ou kouri twòp, ou kase pye ou.
When you run too fast, you stub your foot.
Slow down and be careful or you will make mistakes.

Lè ou rive yon kote, ou danse kou tout moun.
When you go somewhere, dance as everyone does.
When you are a stranger, follow the natives.

Kote ki gen granmoun, kabrit pa mouri nan kòd.
Where there's a grownup, the goat doesn't get strangled on its rope.
Experience prevents mistakes.

Ou mouri; ou mouri pou je ou.
You die; you die for yourself.
Your death brings nothing to anyone else.

Ou pa fouye zo nan kalalou.
You don't look for bones in an okra pod.
Don't search where it's inappropriate.

Ou konn kouri, men fòk ou konn kache.
You know how to run, but you must know how to hide.
You can run, but you can't hide.

Fòk ou konn la pou ou al la.
You must know there to go there.
Experience. You can't do what you don't know.

Ou pa bezwen montre madichon kay.
You don't need to show a curse the way home.
Trouble will find its own way.

Pa rele "fèmen baryè!" lè chwal fin pase.
Don't yell, "Close the gate!" after the horse has gone out.
What's done is done.

Sa ki ta di misye ta mouri jodi a? Fè tan kite tan.
Who would have said that this man would have died today?
Leave time to time.
Don't predict the future. Take things as they come.

Kote ki gen granmoun, kay pa boule.
Where there are grownups, the house doesn't burn down.
Experience prevents mistakes.

Pa joure manman kayiman jouk ou fin pase dlo.
Don't curse the crocodile's mother until you have crossed
the river.
Don't insult your enemies until you are out of danger.

Ou pa gade sou pye bourik pou ou ba l' pote chay.
You don't look at the donkey's legs to give him the load.
Don't ask too many questions.

W'ap fè m' monte nan syèl pa do.
You're making me go to heaven backwards.
You are asking me to do the impossible.

Ou pa pwason; ou pa't pou antre nan nas.
You're not a fish; you shouldn't have entered the net.
You meddled where you didn't belong.

Fòk ou chache konn chemen anvan ou pran wout.
You must learn the way before you take to the road.
Think before you act.

Ou dwe fè ma anvan ou kriye an avan.
You must make a flagstaff before you cry forward.
First things first.

Ou montre makak voye wòch, premye moun li kase tèt se ou menm.
You teach the monkey how to throw rocks and the first person whose head he breaks is yours.
You reap what you sow.

W'ap bay yon karo tè pou yon dan krab.
You're giving an acre of land for a crab claw.
You're being too generous.

Ou poko kenbe chen; ou pa ka di l'ap mouri nan chenn.
You haven't caught the dog; you can't say it'll die on a chain.
Don't count on putting a criminal in jail until you catch him.

Si tèt ou pa travay, pye ou va travay.
If your head doesn't work, your feet will work.
Plan ahead or you will work harder later.

Ou pa pare; pa rele bòs.
You're not ready; don't call the mason/carpenter.
Be patient; don't jump the gun.

Afè ou nan bon ti mamit.
Your affair is in a good little can.
Your business is being taken care of.

Ou poko wè san ou gentan rele jandam.
You have not yet seen blood yet you call the police.
Don't panic so quickly.

Ou nan ka.
You're in a case.
You're in trouble.

Kou ou prese; kafe ou koule ak ma.
When you are in a hurry your coffee has grounds in it.
When you hurry more than you should, you make mistakes.

Lè ou nan abatwa fòk ou aksepte san vole sou ou.
When you are in the slaughterhouse, you must accept blood splattering on you.
When a person hurts others, he will suffer consequences.

Ti poul pa rete dèyè kòk.
Chicks don't follow a rooster.
This is no place for children.

Sansib pa jwe.
Sensitive doesn't gamble.
Gambling is for the tough at heart.

Si ou vle gen rezon devan kras, se benyen pou ou benyen.
If you want to have reason before filth, you must bathe.
You must live right if you want to judge others.

Anvan ou pale gade dèyè.
Before you speak look back.
Take caution before you speak.

"Pa konnen" pa janm al nan prizon.
"Don't know" never goes to jail.
Saying "I don't know" never gets one into trouble.

EXPRESSIONS AND COMMUNICATION

"Bonjou" se paspò ou.
"Good morning" is your passport.

Di se joujou.
Telling is a jewel.

Tout kòd gen de bout.
Every rope has two ends.
Every dispute has two sides.

Di se joujou.
Telling is a jewel.
People love to be the first to tell something.

Sa ki ba ou konsèy achte chwal gwo vant nan tan lapli pa'p ede ou nouri li nan tan sèk.
He who advises you to buy a fat horse during the rainy season won't help you feed it in the dry season.
The ready advisor never wants to accept responsibility for his council.

Tout zanmi gen zanmi.
All friends have friends.
What you tell your friends will get around.

Raje gen zorey.
Weeds have ears.
You think your secret is safe but it is not.

Pawòl anpil mennen kont.
Much talk brings quarrel.
Too much arguing causes conflict.

Manti mèt kouri jan l' kouri; laverite ap kenbe l'.
A lie may run as it may but truth will catch it.
The truth will be known.

Je wè; bouch pe.
Eyes see; the mouth grows quiet.
Seeing is proof. You see and are proven wrong so stop talking.

Lang pa gen dan men li mòde pi rèd.
The tongue has no teeth but it bites harder.
What you say can hurt a person more than a blow.

Rale mennen kase.
Pulling leads to breaking.
Don't force an issue or things may get out of hand.

Sa je pa we bouch pa pale.
What the eye does not see, the mouth does not speak.
You should be certain before speaking.

Fè wè, pa dire.
"I'll show you" doesn't last.
Talking big doesn't last.

"Bonjou" se paspò ou.
"Good morning" is your passport.
Good manners will get you anywhere.

Kout manchèt nan dlo pa gen mak.
A machete blow in the water doesn't make a mark.
The effort is too small to make a difference. Life goes on.

Sa ki fè pwomès bliye, sa k'ap espere sonje.
Those who make promises forget, those who are looking forward remember.
People depend on a promise, which is easy to make, but hard to keep.

Djondjon leve kote l' vle, menm anba jouk poul.
A mushroom springs up where it chooses, even under the chicken roost.
Nothing can prevent little pleasures. (Fresh chicken droppings kill most plants. Mushrooms are delicacies.)

Kochon di wen, men kochon pa janm pale.
A pig says oink, but a pig never speaks.
A person who is talking but saying nothing.

Ankò se repwòch.
Again is a reproach.
A request repeated becomes a complaint.

Mande chemen pa di pèdi pou sa.
Asking the way doesn't mean one is lost.
Asking for advice is not shameful.

Yon sèl moun pa janm pale moun mal.
Just one person never speaks badly about others.
It takes two or more to gossip.

Tout bèt nan lanmè di yo gra; lanbi di l' gra tou.
All the animals in the sea say they're fat; the conch says it's fat, too.
He is only repeating what others say.

Gwo lide, ti memwa.
Big ideas, tiny memory.
All talk and no action.

Gran djòlè dòmi nan prizon.
Big mouths sleep in jail.
Misfortune falls on those who talk too much.

Kozman mande chèz.
Conversation begs a chair.
A good conversation requires sitting down.

Kreyòl pale; Kreyòl konprann.
Creole is spoken; Creole is understood.
Something clearly said and well understood.

Rayi chen; di dan l' blan.
Hate the dog, but say his teeth are white.
Admit the strengths of an enemy.

Merite pa mande.
Deserving doesn't beg.
A person who deserves something should not have to ask for it.

Moun ki di: "Men koulèv la", se li ki touye l'.
The one who says, "Here's the snake," is the one who killed
it.
The informant is responsible for the culprit's punishment.

Bèl pawòl fè rale boutey blanch.
Good stories cause the bottle to be sucked dry.
One forgets what one's doing in the midst of good conversation.

M' pa gen dlo nan bouch mwen.
I have no water in my mouth.
I'm not envious.

Tande pa di konprann pou sa.
Hearing doesn't mean understanding.
Hearing and understanding are two separate things.

Mwen tande l' nan "teledjòl".
I heard it by "telemouth."
Gossip. I heard it through the grapevine.

Si m' di ou, w'a konn pase m'.
If I tell you, you will know more than I do.
Knowledge is power. I can't tell you too much.

Lamepriz vo mye ke repons.
Ignoring is worth more than responding.
Sometimes, no response says the most.

Tande ak wè se de.
Hearing and seeing are two.
Hearing about something is less reliable than witnessing it.

Mande pa vòlè.
Begging is not stealing.
It never hurts to ask.

Bri kouri, nouvèl gaye.
Noise runs, news spreads.
All news gets around but exciting stories spread quickly.

Kite pawòl, pran kantik.
Leave the word; take up the hymn.
Change subjects.

Kite kantik, pran priyè.
Leave the hymn; take up the prayer.
Stop flattering me and tell me what you want.

Nan benyen, pa gen kache lonbrit.
In bathing, there's no hiding the navel.
You have begun to confess so tell the whole truth.

Si chen rakonte w' sa l' wè nan rèv, ou p'ap mache nan nwit.
If the dog tells you what he sees in his dreams, you won't go out at night.
If you knew the truth, you would be afraid.

Se pa tout chen ki jape pou w' vire gade.
It's not every barking dog that you should turn around to look at.
Don't pay attention to every person's criticism.

Se nan chemen ou konnen sak pase nan chanm.
It's on the road that you know what's happening in the bedroom.
Secrets are revealed in public.

Komisyion pa chay.
Messages are not burdens.
It takes no effort to give a message.

Se lè w'ap joure ou konn pawòl ki te kache.
It's when you're arguing that you learn hidden thoughts.
When angry, one may say anything.

Fè koupe fè.
Iron cuts iron.
Even the strong can be hurt.

Kase fèy kouvri sa.
Pluck leaves and cover that.
Let's cover that up.

Lavi se dans kongo.
Life is a Congo dance.
Life follows a fast-paced rhythm, but you never know where it will lead you.

Bouch an bouch, youn di lòt.
Mouth to mouth, one tells another.
News spreads.

Pasyans se gany.
Patience is a possession.
Patience is valuable and it can be lost.

Afè nèg se mistè.
A man's business is a mystery.
One never knows the truth about other people's business.

Se lanmou ki pou geri lanmou.
Love must heal love.
Only a new love makes one forget a lost love.

Sa ki fè pwomès bliye,
sa k'ap espere sonje.
Those who make promises forget,
those who are looking forward remember.

Je wè; bouch pe.
Eyes see; the mouth grows quiet.

Rakonte se vann.
Telling is selling.
Telling one's business is sacrificing one's privacy.

Sèl pa konn vante di l' sale.
Salt doesn't brag that it's salty.
Those who are truly good at what they do don't need to brag.

Wi koupe kont.
Yes cuts a quarrel.
Agreement stops an argument.

Rete koute pi fò pase gwo ble.
Listening is stronger than denim.
A good listener is the best support.

Jwe ak makak, men pa manyen ke l'.
Play with a monkey, but don't touch his tail.
Don't take teasing too far.

Dan griyen pa fè kè kontan.
Grinning teeth don't make a happy heart.
External appearances mask, but they don't change internal feelings.

Se kondisyon ki bat kòk.
Terms are what defeat cocks.
Compromise brings defeat.

Sa ki ret nan kè m' kite m' dòmi lakay.
What remains in my heart allows me to sleep at home.
I am safe because I don't talk too much.

Fòk de son sonnen pou ou konn sa'k genyen legliz.
Two sounds must ring for you to know what's happening at church.
Every bell has two sounds. You don't know the whole story until you have heard both sides.

De je kontre, manti kaba.
Two eyes meet, lying ends.
Face to face, one must tell the truth.

Afè kay moun se mistè.
The affairs of people's homes are a mystery.
Another person's personal business is a secret.

Chat pran lang li.
The cat took his tongue.
He's speechless.

Poul ki kodase pa janm gen ze.
The chicken that clucks never has eggs.
All talk and no action.

Poul ki chante a se li ki ponn.
The chicken that sings is the one that laid the egg.
The person who brags is the one who did the deed.

Bèf di li pral sal savann, se ke l' li sal.
The cow says she's going to dirty the pasture but only soils her tail.
Gossip can backfire.

Koukou wè lwen, li pa wè dèyè tèt li.
The owl sees far; he doesn't see behind his head.
One never knows what goes on behind one's back.

Chen di, "Gade pa twòp".
The dog says, "Watching is not too much."
It does no harm to look.

Chen ki jape pa mòde.
The dog that barks doesn't bite.
All bark and no bite.

Je wè bouch pe.
Eyes see; the mouth is silent.
Proof stops an argument.

Chache kont fasil; se kenbe l' la ki di.
Looking for an argument is easy; it's holding it that's hard.
It is better to reconcile than to hold a grudge.

Rèv chen rete nan kè chen.
The dog's dream remains in his heart.
An evil person does not speak of his schemes.

Tanbou fouye nan bwa, se lakay li vin bat.
A drum is hollowed out in the woods but comes home to be beaten.
Any secret will eventually be made known.

Je pa gen boday.
The eye has no boundaries.
One looks where one pleases.

Kalbas gran bouch pa kenbe dlo.
The large mouthed gourd doesn't hold water.
People who talk too much don't have credibility.

Lonje dwèt se paran souflèt.
The pointed finger is the parent of the slap.
Accusations lead to fights.

Pè pa preche de fwa.
The priest doesn't preach twice.
I will not repeat this warning.

Mayengwen pa janm vle tande li mèg.
The mosquito never wants to hear that he's skinny.
People don't want to hear about their inabilities.

Nanpwen lapriyè ki pa gen amèn.
There's no prayer that doesn't have an amen.
No matter what is said, someone always agrees. It is time to stop asking and move on.

Bouch manje tout manje, men li pa pale tout pawòl.
The mouth eats all foods, but it doesn't speak all words.
Discretion. Some things are not meant to be repeated.

Komisyonè fè pye ou poze, men li pa fè kè ou poze.
Your messenger rests your feet but not your heart.
First-hand knowledge brings the best relief.

Flanm pwazon boule lang ki pale tout pawòl.
The poison flame burns the tongue that speaks everything.
Watch what you say.

Krab sab, twou pa fon.
Sand crab, shallow hole.
Show-offs may talk big, but they don't have much depth.

Pawòl twò fò, machwè gonfle.
Talking too loud swells the jaw.
If you talk too much, you will bring harm to yourself.

Bwa gen zòrèy, sa ki ladan l' se moun.
The forest has ears, what's in it are people.
Watch what you say; eavesdroppers are everywhere.

Kache laverite se antere dlo.
To hide the truth is to bury water.
The truth is always revealed.

Sa je pa wè; pa fè kè tounen.
What the eyes don't see doesn't sour the heart.
What you don't see doesn't bother you. Don't get upset over hearsay.

Nou pa mande pitit samble papa l', nou mande erèz kouch.
We don't ask for the baby to look like his father; we just ask for a happy delivery.
May the project be successful even if it turns out differently than anticipated.

Gen kose, men nanpwen tan.
There's conversation but no time.
There is much to say, but no time in which to say it.

Gade pa boule je.
Looking doesn't burn the eyes.
It doesn't hurt to look.

Twòp lespri fè yon nonm sòt
Too much intelligence makes a man stupid.
A person can be highly educated but impractical.

Ou mèt filozòf jan ou filozòf; ou pa ka ekri "oum koun koun".
You may be a great philosopher but you can't write "oum koun koun."
Thinking doesn't bring about doing. You are intelligent but impractical.

Pawòl gen pye.
Words have feet.
Word will travel.

Sa ki nan tèt mwen, li pa nan pye mwen.
What's in my head is not in my feet.
One can't always carry out one's thoughts.

Lè yo vle touye yon chen, yo di l' fou.
When they want to kill a dog, they say it's mad.
Intentional false rumors are used to discredit someone.

W'ap mande simityè si l' pa bezwen mò.
You're asking the cemetery if it doesn't need the dead.
The answer is obvious. You don't need to ask that.

Pawòl nan vant pa pouri trip.
Words in the stomach don't rot the intestines.
Not saying something doesn't hurt you.

Fòk ou gen pasyans pou ou leve solèy.
You must have patience to raise the sun.
It takes patience to do a big job.

Ou kite kote kò a ye; ou al kriye kote sèkèy la ye.
You leave the body to mourn at the coffin.
It is too late to tell someone how you feel after they have died.
Also used to mean that you are asking the wrong person for
something.

Fòk ou bat tanbou a pou tande son l'.
You must beat the drum to hear its sound.
You must talk to people to know what they're like.

Se pa ou ki di ou verite.
It is your own who tell you the truth.
Others will flatter you, but those who love you will tell you the
truth.

Konn li pa di lespri pou sa.
Knowing how to read does not mean you have wisdom.
The level of education of a person is not a proof of intelligence.

Lang ou pa lanmè, men li ka neye ou.
Your tongue is not the sea, but it can drown you.
What you say can harm you.

Misye ap benyen chen.
The fellow is bathing dogs.
He is helping the ungrateful.

Mize pote bon nouvèl.
Take time to bring good news.
Stick it out and get the job done.

Wè pi bon pase tande.
Seeing is better than hearing.
Proof of seeing for yourself.

Djòl fè dèt, dèyè peye l'.
The mouth makes a debt; the behind pays it.
A scapegoat pays for other's misdeeds.

Pa mouri, pa jete.
Not dead, don't discard.
You never know when something or someone will be useful or helpful.

Yon sèl zèl pa vole.
One wing doesn't fly.
We need each other.

Se pitit ki kriye ki jwen tete.
The crying baby is the one who gets the breast.
Unless you ask you don't receive.

Se anvi bay ki bay.
It's the desire to give that gives.
True giving comes from the heart. We give to others because we want to give and to be generous.

Ou fòse bourik janbe dlo, men ou pa fòse l' bwè.
You can make a donkey cross the creek, but you can't make it drink.
You can force people to do some things but not others.

Ti bwa pliye. Gwo bwa kase.
The little tree bends. The big tree breaks.
Young people learn new things more easily than the elderly.

Joure kote ou prale pa kote ou soti.
Curse the place you are going to, not where you came from.
Speak well of those you know and who know you. You may need them in the future.

Avan poul vole, se ta li fè.
Before the hen flies, she curtsies.
Mind your manners.

Se siwo ki rale foumi.
It's honey that draws ants.
Kindness accomplishes more than meanness.

Fòse moun fè sa yo pa vle fè se tankou eseye plen lanmè ak wòch.
Forcing people do what they don't want to do is like trying to fill the ocean with rocks.
You can't force people to go against their will.

Jan ou vini se jan yo resevwa ou.
The way you come is how you are received.
One's manners dictate one's treatment.

Lajan fèt pou konte.
Money is made for counting.
Proper accountability serves both parties.

Loraj pa lapli.
Thunder is not rain.
All talk no action.

Twou manti pa fon.
The hole of a lie isn't deep.
You don't have to look far for the truth to be revealed.

Pye mache dèyè kè.
Feet follow the heart.
Following love. Home is where the heart is.

Friends, Family and Relationships

Tout venn touche kè.
All veins touch the heart.

Yon bon zanmi pi bon pase frè.
A good friend is better than a brother.

Yon bon mari dwe soud e yon bon madanm dwe avèg.
A good husband should be deaf, and a good wife should be blind.
A husband should not listen to everything his wife says, and a wife should not scrutinize everything her husband does.

Bèf pa janm bouke pote kòn li.
A cow never tires of carrying her horns.
You never get tired of caring for your own.

Joumou pa janm donnen kalbas.
A pumpkin never bears gourds.
Children are like their parents.

Bèl dan pa di zanmi pou sa.
Beautiful teeth do not mean friendship.
A smiling person is not necessarily a friend.

Timoun pa chen, granmoun pa Bondyè.
Children aren't dogs, adults aren't God.
Treat others with respect, and remember that nobody is perfect.

Kras ki sou do kay se li ki tonbe nan citèn.
The dirt that is on the roof is what falls into the cistern.
Children learn bad ways from their parents.

Koupe kann bay zanmi souse.
Cutting sugar cane for your friends to suck.
You are doing the work, but your friends are living off of you.

Frape je nen kouri dlo. Frape nen je kouri dlo.
Strike the eye, the nose runs. Strike the nose, the eye runs.
What hurts a loved one hurts you, too.

Dwèt ou fè ou mal, ou pa jete l'.
Your finger hurts you but you don't throw it away.
A family member may do wrong, but you don't disown him.

Yon bon zanmi pi bon pase frè.
A good friend is better than a brother.
A true friend will serve you better than family.

Timoun ki kriye nan kay ak sa ki kriye nan pòt se menm.
The child who cries in the house and the one who cries at the door are the same.
Treat other people's children as you treat your own.

Manman poul di: mwen ka pale pou ze mwen, men mwen pa ka pale pou ti poul mwen.
The hen says: I can speak for my eggs, but not for my chicks.
A parent cannot promise how a child will develop.

Ou pa kapab kouche sou nat pou ap pale nat mal.
You can't sleep on the mat and speak badly about the mat.
Don't speak poorly of those who are helping you.

Tout venn touche kè.
All veins touch the heart.
What affects your family affects you.

"Padon" pa geri maleng.
"Sorry" doesn't heal a sore.
Feeling sorry doesn't right a wrong.

Bouch ki karese fanm se li ki mete l' deyò.
The mouth that caresses a woman is the one that puts her out.
A man is kind to a woman to court her but not always after he has won her.

Pitit deyò toujou sanble papa.
A bastard child always looks like his father.
You can't hide your mistakes.

Sa ki kouche ak chen, se li ki leve ak pis.
He who lies with dogs rises with fleas.
Bad influences lead to bad character.

Lougawou nan fanmi mal pou rekonèt.
A werewolf in the family is hard to recognize.
One does not want to notice the evil in one's own family.

Doktè pa janm trete tèt li.
A doctor never treats himself.
You always need someone else to help you.

Chen pa janm mòde pitit li jouk nan zo.
A dog never bites her young to the bone.
A mother doesn't punish her children too severely.

Men ale, men vini fè zanmi dire.
A hand going out, a hand coming back makes a friendship last.
Helping each other makes a friendship last.

Tout venn pou san.
All veins are for blood.
Relatives stick together.

Yon pitit ka gen anpil papa men yon sèl manman.
A child can have many fathers, but can have only one mother.
The mother is always known. Some things are uncertain but we know this much for sure.

Fòk ou konn manje pawòl pou ou gen zanmi.
You must know how to eat words to have friends.
You must know how to apologize to keep your friends.

Chen anraje mòde menm mèt li.
A rabid dog even bites its master.
A person who has lost his temper will hurt those close to him.

Achte, peye; prete, remèt. Men sa ki fè yon nonm.
Buy, pay; borrow, return. This is what makes a man.
Paying one's dues brings one respect.

Pitit se richès malere.
Children are the wealth of the poor.
One's hope and riches lie in the future of one's children.

Moun pa se dra.
A friend is a sheet.
Friends cover for each other.

Byen pre pa lakay.
Close is not home.
Almost is not as good as arriving. There's no place like home.

Papa pitit toujou gen tach sou kanson l'.
A father always has stains on his pants.
Children make mistakes which affect their parents.

Yon sèl kabrit gate bann.
A single goat spoils the herd.
A person with bad habits influences those associated with him.

Depi ou nan lafanmi djondjon fòk dan ou nwa.
As long as you're in the djondjon (black mushroom) family,
your teeth will be black.
One always resembles one's associates.

Pitit pa janm mouri pou manman. Se manman ki mouri pou pitit.
Children never die for their mothers. Mothers are the ones
who die for their children.
A mother will sacrifice all for her children.

Moun pa ou se moun pa ou nèt.
A buddy is a buddy all the way.
Friendship is forever.

Kamarad fè pann.
Comrades get you hung.
Bad friendships bring trouble.

Pa janm jete vye chodyè pou nèf.
Never discard an old pot for a new one.
Don't abandon old friends when you make new ones.

Chak bourik ranni nan patiraj li.
Each donkey brays in its pasture.
At home, one is free to do as one pleases.

Kamarad sove ou.
Comrades save you.
True friends watch out for each other.

Rad sal lave nan fanmi.
Dirty clothes are washed in the family.
Don't expose your personal problems to the public.

Pa pouse m'; m'a mache.
Don't push me; I'll walk.
Don't force me; I know what to do.

Pa jete vye chodyè; w'a bezwen l' ankò.
Don't throw away the old kettle; you'll need it again.
One will always need an old friend.

Bwè dlo nan vè; respekte vè.
Drink water from the glass; respect the glass.
Respect those who help you.

Menm nan lanfè gen moun pa.
Even in hell there are buddies.
There is always someone to give you a hand.

Tout moun genyen yon bwa anba bannann yo.
Everybody has a stake under his banana stalk.
We all need a little help.

Si andedan pa vann ou, deyò pa ka achte ou.
If inside doesn't sell you, outside can't buy you.
If the insiders don't betray a person, their enemies can't get them.

Tout moun konnen kouto pa janm grate manch pa li.
Everybody knows that a knife never scrapes its own handle.
You must have help for some things.

A defo'd chen, kabrit al lachas.
For a lack of dogs, goats go hunting.
In difficult times you use what you have out of necessity.

Si ou pa lakay ou, ou pa granmoun.
If you are not at home, you're not an adult.
You can only do as you wish at home.

Si ou te chen m', m' ta mache san baton.
If you were my dog, I'd walk without a stick.
If you were my companion, I would have no fear.

Si pa te gen bourik, pa ta gen milèt.
If there were no donkeys, there would be no mules.
A small thing may bring about something more important.
Parents work hard so their children can get ahead.

De mòn pa janm kontre, men de kretyen vivan ka kontre.
Two mountains never meet, but two human beings can meet.
We are human; we can come to an agreement.

Mwen vin bwè lèt; mwen pa vin konte ti bèf.
I come to drink milk; I don't come to count calves.
I'm here to enjoy what you have, not to ask you how you got it.
I'm not checking up on you.

Règleman pa gate zanmi.
Settling up doesn't spoil a friendship.
Settling up finances prevents resentment.

Si ou manje ak moun, manje ou pa janm fini.
If you eat with people, your food is never finished.
Those who share receive in return and never run out. (Eat with people means to share food.)

Si ou gen yon sous kap ba ou dlo, ou pa koupe bwa kote l'.
If you have a spring that's giving you water, you don't cut the trees around it.
Protect those who help you.

Si ou nan rejiman bourik, fò'k ou pote ba.
If you're in a regiment of donkeys, you must carry a pack saddle.
When you join a group, you must carry part of the load. You must do as those around you do.

Maladi kanmarad pa anpeche kanmarad li dòmi.
The illness of a friend doesn't keep his friend from sleeping.
There is only so much you can do for a friend.

Zafè ti poul, moun pa mele.
In the affairs of the baby chick, people don't interfere.
Mind your own business.

Se chat kay k'ap manje poul kay.
It's the house cat that is eating the household chickens.
It's an insider job.

Se lè ou malad pou ou konnen si ou gen zanmi.
It's when you are sick that you know if you have friends.
True friends see one through the hard times.

Fè zanmi ak kouto anvan abriko mi.
Make friends with the knife before the fruit is ripe.
Prepare for opportunity.

Se kolòn ki bat.
It's the column (of soldiers) who win.
Those who stick together accomplish more.

Se pasajè ki tann machin.
It's the passengers that wait for the car.
The leader is in control.

Ti rat pa janm fèt san ke.
Little rats are never born without tails.
Heritage. A person who comes from a bad family.

Lanmou pa konn dèyè pyese.
Love doesn't see patched trousers.
True love doesn't care about flaws.

Nan dinen malfini, ou manje koulèv.
At the hawk's dinner, you eat snakes.
One must swallow the consequences of the company one keeps.

Se lè ou nan bezwen, ou konn ki moun ki zanmi ou.
It's when you are in need that you know your friends.
A friend in need is a friend indeed.

Gad nan pa ou.
Look in yours.
Mind your own business.

Se nan menaj ou konn bon fanm.
It's in the housekeeping that you know a good woman.
People who are there for you when you need them.

Tanga pi rèd pase rad.
Old rags are tougher than good clothes.
Old friends are better than new ones.

Mennen koulèv lekòl pa anyen, se fè l' chita ki rèd.
Taking a snake to school is nothing; it's making him sit
that's tough.
*Telling someone something is easy; the challenge lies in getting
him to do what you want.*

Bèlmè pa manman; bòpè pa papa.
Mother-in-law is not mother; father-in-law is not father.
Parents are irreplaceable. A substitute is never as good.

Vwazinaj se fanmi.
Neighbors are family.
*Good neighbors are like family. What one wants for one's
family, one should want for one's neighbors.*

Pa sèvi pè ou, ou kite pitit ou mouri chwal.
Not serving your priest, you let your child die like a horse.
Your unethical actions bring retribution on your family.

Chodyè prete pa kreve pwa sèk.
The borrowed pot won't cook dried beans.
Borrowed things must not be kept too long.

Sonje premye lapli ki te leve mayi.
Remember the first rain that sprouted the corn.
Remember those who helped in the beginning.

Bò papa se pètèt; bò manman se sèten.
On the father's side it's maybe; on the mother's side it's
certain.
*One is always sure of the identity of the mother. A mother is
more likely to grant a wish.*

Di mwen sa ou frekante; m'a di ou sa ou ye.
Tell me the company you keep; I'll tell you what you are.
One can know a person by his/her associates.

Se kouto sèl ki konnen sa ki nan kè yanm.
Only the knife knows what is in the heart of the yam.
Difficult times reveal a person's true character.

Leve m' wo, mete m' ba.
Lift me high, put me low.
Do with me as you please.

Plimen poul la men pa kite l' rele.
Pluck the chicken but don't let it squawk.
To take advantage of someone in a way that they don't realize what is being done to them.

Sa foumi genyen, se sa l' bay pitit li.
What the ant gives her baby is what she has.
A mother gives her children what she can.

Fè respè ou; m'a fè pa m'.
Show your respect; I'll show mine.
Respect must be mutual.

Baton ede pye.
The cane helps the foot.
Someone to lean on makes the going easier.

Bourik fè pitit pou do l' ka poze.
The donkey bears foal so its back can rest.
Children must help their parents.

Pitit mouri nan men manman l' pa gen repwòch.
There is no reproach when the child dies in his mother's hands.
There is no blame when a person damages something that belongs to them.

Se lanmou ki pou geri lanmou.
Love must heal love.

Manman poul di: mwen ka pale pou ze mwen,
men mwen pa ka pale pou ti poul mwen.
The hen says: I can speak for my eggs,
but not for my chicks.

Chen ki konnen ou, se li ki souke ke l' pou ou.
The dog that knows you is the one that wags his tail for you.
People are more likely to do favors for those they know.

Kabrit mawon rekonèt pye kamarad li.
The wild goat recognizes its comrade's tracks.
One recognizes one's own, even under disguise.

Bèf pa janm di savann li pa bezwen l'.
The cow never tells the pasture she doesn't need it.
Be kind to those who help you.

Jou ou pare, ou pa kontre ak bèlmè ou.
On the day that you are ready, you don't meet up with your mother-in-law.
Unpleasant encounters seem to always take one by surprise.

Kapon touye manman l'.
The coward kills his mother.
Fear makes one hurt those one loves.

Baton fanmi pa janm kase.
The family walking cane is never broken.
Family members are always there for each other.

Zafè kabrit pa zafè mouton.
The goat's business is not the sheep's business.
Mind your own business.

Madichon koukou pa touye frize, men li degrese l'.
The cuckoo's curse may not kill the owl, but it can make him loose weight.
Hatred from others causes stress.

Chodyè ou pa monte, ou pa desann li.
If you didn't put the kettle on the fire don't take it off.
Don't meddle in other people's quarrels.

Mennaj pa bon men li itil.
Having a mistress isn't good, but it's useful.
Expediency. Everyone serves a purpose.

Tanbou bat nan raje, men se lakay li vin danse.
The drum beats in the underbrush, but it dances at home.
You work in public and relax at home.

Bon chwal vann dèyè manman l'.
The good colt is sold behind its mother.
Reputation counts. Good things don't last.

Krapo pa gen lapenn pou dèyè l' kap frape atè; se pa mwen ki pou gen lapenn pou li.
The frog doesn't worry about his behind hitting the ground; I shouldn't fret for him either.
Don't worry about what doesn't bother others.

Kout pye jiman pa touye poulen.
The mare's kick doesn't kill the colt.
A mother is never too harsh with her children.

Chodyè ki pa bouyi pou ou, ou pa dekouvri l'.
Don't uncover a kettle that isn't boiling for you.
Stay out of other people's affairs.

Se mèt lanmò ki veye mò l'.
The master of death watches over its dead.
The family takes care of its own problems.

Tcherache pa janm fè pitit ak tche.
Those whose tails (roots) have been pulled out never give birth to children with tails (roots).
Children are like their parents. A" tcherache" is a prostitute and is not expected to have a respectable daughter.

Ti mapou pa grandi anba gwo mapou.
A little mapou doesn't grow under a big mapou tree.
One can't develop under another person's shadow.

Ti bourik pa kouri pase manman l'.
The little donkey doesn't run faster than its mother.
One is only as good as one's roots.

Makak karese pitit li jouk li touye l'.
The monkey caresses her baby to death.
Over protection. Or good intentions turned out badly.

Mayengwen danse, men li pa bliye janm li.
The mosquito dances, but it doesn't forget its legs.
Celebrate your success, but don't forget those who have helped you.

Matla fè banda tout tan dra pa kouvri l'.
The mattress runs wild as long as the sheet doesn't cover it.
Having fun when the boss or parents are absent.

Bèlmè pa janm gen bon do.
The mother-in-law never has a good back.
The mother-in-law is always criticized behind her back.

Nen pran kou; je kouri dlo.
The nose takes the blow; the eyes run with water.
When misfortune strikes one member of the family, the others also suffer.

Moun ki dòmi ak Jan, se li konnen si Jan wonfle.
The one who sleeps with John is the one who knows if John snores.
To know someone's wrong doings, you must be involved.

Tout machann gen de mezi.
Every vendor has two measures.
People treat their friends better than others.

Se soulye ki konnen si chosèt gen twou.
Only the shoe knows if the sock has holes.
Those who know a secret must be involved too.

Mèt do pa grate do.
You don't scratch your own back.
One always needs help from others.

Jako pa janm bliye premye mèt li.
A parrot never forgets its first master.
One never forgets one's first teacher.

Moun ki swe pou ou, se pou li ou chanje chemiz.
You only change your shirt for one who sweats for you.
Your obligation is to the one who helps you.

Lafimen pa janm mete mèt kay deyò.
Smoke never chases out the owner of the house.
A person does not see his own faults or those of his family.

Kiyè al kay granmèl, se pou granmèl al kay kiyè tou.
The spoon goes to the house of the wooden bowl; the wooden bowl must also go to the house of the spoon.
People must help those who help them.

Pitit tig se tig.
The tiger's cub is a tiger.
Like father like son.

Yanm swiv gòl.
The yam vine follows the pole.
The disciple will follow the example set by the master.

Zanmi ou ankouraje ou tann manje pare men li p'ap mache ak ou nan nwit.
Your friend encourages you to wait for supper to cook, but he won't walk you home in the night.
Friendship when it is easy but not when it is difficult.

Lang ak dan pa janm mòde.
The tongue and teeth never bite each other.
When you live in close proximity with others, live in peace.

Nanpwen chodyè pou bouyi move fanmi.
There's no pot to boil bad relatives.
One is stuck with one's family.

Yo pa ka achte moso manman nan mache.
One can't buy a piece of mother in the market.
Mothers are irreplaceable.

Moun sa yo se Kòkòt ak Figaro.
Those people are Kòkòt and Figaro.
They are inseparable friends.

Moun sa yo se lèt ak sitwon.
Those people are milk and lime.
People who cannot get along together.

Sa ki pase nan kizin, lakay pa bezwen konen l'.
What happens in the kitchen, the house doesn't need to know.
Please keep this conversation private.

Lè ravèt vle fè dans, li pa janm envite poul.
When the cockroach wants to have a dance, he doesn't invite the chicken.
One doesn't socialize with one's enemies.

Sa chat konnen se li li montre pitit li.
What the cat knows is what she teaches her kittens.
Parents teach what they know to their children.

Lè vant plen, pitit toujou sanble papa.
When the stomach is full, the child always looks like the father.
When things are going well everyone takes credit.

Fanm pou yon tan, manamn pou tout tan.
Wife for a while, mother forever.
A mother is forever.

Lè w'ap manje ak dyab, ou kenbe kiyè ou long.
When eating with the Devil, hold your spoon out far.
Take caution when dealing with evil people.

Sa manman poul gaye, se sa pitit li manje.
What the hen scratches up is what the chicks eat.
Children pay the consequences of their parents' actions.

Sa kaptenn batiman te di anlè, se li li di atè.
What the ship's captain said at sea is what he says on land.
The leader's word is final.

Lè ou fè nèg byen se manman ou ou kale.
When you do good for others, it's your mother you beat.
Help family; strangers will be ungrateful.

Lè ou gen pitit fi, ou pa janm ka di kochon pa'p monte tab ou.
When you have daughters, you can never say that pigs won't sit at your table.
You have to take the son-in-law your daughter brings to you.

Ou kouche sou po bèf la epi w'ap pale bèf la mal.
You sleep on cowhide, yet you speak badly of the cow.
Don't speak poorly of those who help you.

Lè ou pa gen pitit, ou se chen.
When you have no children, you are a dog.
One's children determine one's worth.

Ou se papiyon; mwen se lanp.
You are a moth; I am a lamp.
You will always come to me.

Lè gen twòp makomè, non an gate.
When there are too many girlfriends, the name is spoiled.
More promises have been made than can be kept.

Lè w'ap benyen pitit lòt moun, lave yon bò, kite yon bò.
When you are bathing someone else's baby, wash one side
and leave one side.
*Don't be overly critical of other people's children. Overlook some
things.*

Granmesi chen se kout baton.
A dog's thanks is a beating.
Ingratitude.

Bourik je fon kriye bonè.
A donkey with deep eyes cries early.
*People with deep emotions are hurt more easily. Those who see
the most, hurt the soonest.*

Nan fè bren, raje se lougawou.
At night bushes are warewolves.
Things seem worse when we are afraid.

Rad ki tache mete jouk li chire.
A stained dress is worn until it wears out.
*You must live a long time with the consequences of your
mistakes.*

Tan pare pa di lapli pou sa.
A gathering storm doesn't necessarily mean rain.
Impending danger may not mean disaster.

Se apre batay ou konte blese.
It's after the battle that you count the wounded.
Don't give up until the end.

Lè w'ap bwè nan yon sous, ou pa kaka ladan l'.
When you drink from a spring, you don't shit in it.
Don't criticize those who help you.

Maladi pa konn vanyan.
Illness doesn't know the strong.
Sickness and misfortune can come to anyone.

Se lè ou pase maladi ou konnen remèd.
It's when you've been sick that you know medicine.
Experience.

Moun ou konnen la jounen nan fè nwa ou pa bezwen klere chandel pou ou rekonèt li.
You don't need to light a candle at night to recognize a person you know during the day.
Friends are never strangers.

Kote zonbi konnen ou, li pa fè ou pè.
Where the zombie knows you, he won't frighten you.
Even evildoers need friends.

Ou se tèt koupe ak papa ou.
You are the cut off head of your father.
You look just like your father.

Bèlmè ou pa bat ou, men li regle ou nan kwi ou.
Your mother-in-law doesn't beat you, but she fixes you in your food bowl.
The mother-in-law will always have the last word.

Achte kochon pou ras.
Buy the hog for its bloodline.
One is only as good as one's roots.

HUMAN BEHAVIOR

Bale nèf bale byen.
A new broom sweeps well.

Ti gason ki monte bwa pa granmoun pou sa.
Climbing a tree does not a make a little boy a man.

Ti gason ki monte bwa pa granmoun pou sa.
Climbing a tree does not a make a little boy a man.
Experience, not position, makes a person.

Twal sal fasil men mal pou lave.
Cloth soils easily but is difficult to wash.
It is easier to loose one's reputation than to regain it.

Fanm gen fòs nan bouch, gason gen fòs nan men.
Woman has strength in the mouth, man has strength in the hand.
Women talk too much, and men resort too quickly to violence.

Vòlè pa bay kanmarad li pote gwo sak.
A thief doesn't give his mate a big sack to carry.
The guilty do not trust others.

Lavi long se plis lespri.
A long life is more sense.
The longer you live, the wiser you become.

Rat kay manje pay kay.
The house rat eats the roof straw.
It was an inside job.

Nan move van malfini ak poul jouke sou menm pye bwa.
In a hurricane the hawk and the chicken roost on the same tree.
When faced with a greater danger, enemies must work together.

Se pa tout moun ki ale legliz pou priye.
Not everyone goes to church to pray.
You cannot know another person's motives.

Mwen ba w' sal w'ap mande salon.
I give you a room and now you want the living room.
People are never satisfied.

Bale nèf bale byen.
A new broom sweeps well.
A employee works harder when first employed.

Chat kenbe rat men li vòlè pwason mèt li.
A cat catches rats but steals its master's fish.
A person is capable of both good and evil.

Tout manyòk gen menm po men yo pa gen menm gou.
All cassavas have the same skin but they don't have the same taste.
People may be dressed the same but they are different in their ways.

Granmoun se remèd.
Old people are a remedy. Age is medicine.
The elderly are full of useful wisdom.

Se pa paske chen an jwe avè' w' ke li pa'p mòde w'.
It is not because the dog plays with you that he won't bite you.
Some people act kindly but will hurt you if given an opportunity.

Pye chat dous men zong li move.
The cat's foot is soft but it's claws are mean.
A warning when things appear better than they are.

Kabrit anpil mèt mouri grangou nan solèy.
The goat of many owners dies hungry in the sun.
A group-owned item is never well cared for.

Zoranj la mi men se kouto ki di si li dous.
The orange is ripe but the knife tells if it is sweet.
It looks good but you won't know its value until you put it to the test.

Move zafè pa janm gen mèt.
A mess never has an owner.
Nobody wants to take responsibility for a bad situation.

Se anpil dlo ki lave kay tè.
It takes a lot of water to wash a mud hut.
It is difficult to change the ways of country folk.

Bèf nan poto pa pè kouto.
A cow tied to the stake (for a fine) doesn't fear the knife.
I'm not worried. I know that you won't punish me too badly. At poto means that the animal is held by the sheriff for a fine, not to be butchered.

Se kouto ki di sa ki nan vant joumou.
It is the knife that says what is in the belly of the pumpkin.
You can't judge by appearances. People must be put to the test.

Bèl fanm se traka.
A beautiful woman is trouble.
A woman who relies on her looks is trouble.

Bonjou fanm pa laverite.
A woman's "good morning" is not the truth.
She does not mean what she is saying.

Gade pa pete je.
Looking doesn't make you blind.
It does't hurt to look.

Apre fèt grate tèt.
After the party, scratch the head.
Frivolous actions have consequences.

Djòl fanm pa gen dimanch.
A woman's yap has no Sunday.
A woman never rests from talking.

Ti kouri, kenbe tete; gwo kouri lage tete.
When you run, hold your breasts. When you flee drop your breasts.
In great danger you forget everything.

Bon fanm pa rantre nan pòch.
A good wife doesn't go into pockets.
A good wife doesn't ask for too much money.

Li di "prete m'", men li vle di "ban m'".
He says, "lend me," but he means, "give me."
Borrowers are beggars.

Lontan se kochon ki te konn di "rm, rm". Jodi a se moun kap di "rm, rm".
A long time ago, it was the pig that used to grunt "rm, rm."
Today people are grunting "rm, rm."
Good manners are less common and people are acting more and more like animals.

Remèd timoun radi se fwèt.
A naughty child's medicine is a switch.
A spanking is the cure for a misbehaved child.

Kaka je pa linèt.
Eye crud is not glasses.
What is being done does not help, but there is something that will.

Tout zetwal klere, men tout zetwal pa klere menn jan.
All stars shine, but not all stars shine the same way.
They all may look good, but some are better than others.

Tout fanm se fanm, men tout fanm pa menm.
All women are women, but not all women are the same.
This can be used either as a criticism or as a compliment.

Bat men ankouraje chen.
Clapping hands encourages the dog.
Attention gives encouragement.

Tout tan tèt pa koupe, ou pa di li p'ap bliye chapo.
As long as he doesn't loose his head, don't say he won't forget his hat.
Anything is still possible.

Mande poul pouki sa li pa dòmi sou palmis.
Ask the chicken why it doesn't sleep on a palm tree.
Something that is beyond a person's abilities.

Bèl flè san zodè.
Beautiful flower without a scent.
A beautiful person who has no sense.

Vyann mouri pa pè santi.
Dead meat is not afraid to stink.
The dead have no fears. One who has nothing to lose.

Bèl fanm, bèl malè.
Beautiful woman, beautiful misfortune.
A beautiful woman can cause great problems.

Timoun se bèt.
Children are beasts.
Children act more like animals than people.

Chak chen pipi jan l' konnen.
Every dog pees the way it knows.
One acts the way one knows to behave.

Tout tan tèt poko koupe, li pa dekouraje pote chapo.
As long as the head is not yet cut off, it isn't discouraged from wearing a hat.
Old habits die hard.

Granmoun pa monte chwal bwa.
An adult doesn't ride a hobbyhorse.
Adults don't play around.

Bay kou bliye; pote mak sonje.
He who strikes the blow, forgets; he who bears the bruise, remembers.
The victim never forgets.

Granmoun pa tounen timoun.
Adults don't become children.
Act your age.

Bon karaktè se wanga fanm lèd.
Good character is the ugly woman's magic charm.
Character is more important than looks. The situation is better than it looks.

Graje manyòk, nanpwen konpayi; kasav sou platen, gen rejiman.
When grating the cassava, there is no company; when the cassava is on the griddle, there is a regiment.
Nobody wants to help with the work, but all want to enjoy the end product.

Si yon fanm neglijan, fòk li malpwòp.
If a woman is negligent, she must be unclean.
An irresponsible person doesn't take care of him/herself.

Nan fè bren moun pè bri rat.
In the dark, people fear the rat's noise.
People fear the unknown.

Se yon bon katolik ki fè yon bon pwotestan.
It takes a good Catholic to make a good Protestant.
A dedicated person will always do right.

Se anpil dlo ki lave kay tè.
It takes a lot of water to wash a mud hut.

Fanm gen fòs nan bouch, gason gen fòs nan men.
Woman has strength in the mouth,
man has strength in the hand.

Si bouzen te tanpe, anpil fanm ta kache.
If whores were branded, many women would hide.
If you only knew the truth. Many people have secrets.

Pito yo ba ou veye yon barik rat, pase yo ba ou veye ti fi.
Better to watch over a barrel of rats than little girls.
Little girls are trouble.

Si bèf te konnen fòs li, li pa ta kite fanm mennen l'.
If the cow knew its strength, it wouldn't let a women lead it.
The strong let the weak lead them out of ignorance.

Mwen se kiyè bwa; m' pa pè chalè.
I'm a wooden spoon; I'm not afraid of heat.
I'm not afraid of a situation or what is being said about me.

Si syèl te tonbe, yo ta ramase zetwal.
If the sky fell, they would pick up stars.
They'll take anything.

Si ou tande plenn ti mal, ou ta di l'ap pote yon barik sèl.
If you heard the complaints of the little man, you'd say he's carrying a barrel of salt.
He's exaggerating his complaints.

Se nan chemen jennen yo kenbe chwal malin.
It's in a narrow path that they catch a cunning horse.
You must corner him before he will admit the truth.

Twò konnen fè avèg koupe makak li twò kout.
Knowing too much makes the blind man cut his cane too short.
The "know-it-all" gets himself into trouble.

Se sourit ki montre twou li.
It's the mouse that shows its hole.
A person leads the way to their downfall.

Nan mare baryè timoun kale granmoun.
In the tying of the gate the child beats the adult.
It's harder to keep young people at home than adults.

Se lè koulèv mouri ou wè longè l'.
It's when the snake dies that you see its length.
A person's guard is not let down until after death.

Y'ap kondwi Bouki de bra dèyè pou dèt; l'ap machande ak pye.
Because of debt, they are leading Bouki away with his arms behind his back but he's bargaining with his feet.
A borrower never runs out of stories and excuses.

Twòp lespri, sòt pa lwen.
Too smart, stupidity is not far.
The very intelligent are often impractical.

Se nan men yo kenbe vòlè.
It's in-hand they catch a thief.
You must catch him in the act.

Avoka se sizo, se sa ki nan mitan yo koupe.
Lawyers are scissors, they cut out the middle.
Lawyers are the only ones who come out winners.

Chache fanm pa mal; se pwovizyon ki rèd.
Looking for women isn't bad; it's providing provisions that's hard.
The consequences are the true price of one's actions.

Plis chen, plis pis.
More dogs, more fleas.
More children, more problems.

Gason konn bouke, men pa fanm.
Men get tired, but not women.
Woman's work never ends.

Lanmò manman yon moun, se kout tafya yon lòt.
The death of one person's mother provides drink for
another.
One man's sorrow is another man's joy.

Bèl dan pa kè.
Pretty teeth are not heart.
Outward beauty is not inward beauty. Deceitful intentions.

Memwa se paswa.
Memory is a sieve.
It's easy to forget things.

Lajan pa janm ase pou fanm.
Money is never enough for a woman.
Women always want more money.

Moun ki p'ap peye toujou ap achte kredi.
People who won't pay are always buying on credit.
Borrowers don't pay their dues.

Brav pa konn nan nwit.
The brave don't know nighttime.
A person who knows no fear.

Meyè gad kò se je.
The best bodyguard is the eye.
One's own awareness is the best defense.

Dòmi pa konn mizè.
Sleep knows no misery.
Sleep brings peace and quiet.

Dòmi se ti frè lanmò.
Sleeping is death's younger brother.
In sleep, one is dead to the world.

Bèf dèyè bwè pi bon dlo.
The last cow drinks the best water.
You are more comfortable when no one is pushing you.

Bèf dèyè bwè dlo sal.
The last cow drinks dirty water.
When you come late you get second choice.

Chwal konn longè kòd li.
The horse knows the length of his rope.
People know how much they can get away with.

Moun chich toujou renmen bagay moun.
Stingy people always like other people's things.
Stingy people don't want to use their own things.

Ou se kokoye.
You are a coconut.
A person who has nice words but who is not generous. A hard nut to crack.

Tèt ki te bliye chapo ap toujou bliye chapo.
The head that forgot the hat will always forget the hat.
Old habits persist.

Se maten manchèt timoun file.
The child's machete is sharpened in the morning.
The inexperienced don't plan ahead.

Bourik toujou aji tankou bourik.
The donkey always acts like a donkey.
You can't change a person's nature.

Chen manjè d' ze pa janm kite metye l'.
The egg-eating dog never leaves its trade.
Bad behavior and habits are not easily changed.

Bouch granmoun santi, men pawòl li dous.
Old people's mouths stink but their words are sweet.
An old person is full of wisdom.

Sitwon vèt konn tonbe kite sitwon mi.
The green lime can fall, leaving the ripe lime.
Sometimes the young die and leave the old behind.

Machann lèt se rizièz.
The milk vendor is a sly one. (You can't tell if she has watered down the milk.)
You can't tell what she is up to.

Kochon benyen nan labou; se gou l'.
The pig bathes in mud; it's his taste.
To each his own.

Ti kochon mande manman li: Ki sa ki fè bouch ou long konsa? Manman kochon reponn li: Se vini w'ap vini - wa gentan wè.
The piggy asks his mama: What is it that makes you so sad? The mama pig tells him: You're just coming along - you'll see soon enough.
With age comes wisdom. If you only knew what lies ahead.

Ti chen gen fòs devan kay mèt li.
The puppy is courageous in front of his master's house.
The young feel brave at home. A weak person is brave if he has a powerful protector.

Larivyè pa janm gwosi san l' pa twouble.
The river never swells without being troubled.
Change brings temporary discomfort.

Moun sòt se levenman
A fool is an event.
A foolish person is entertaining.

Sa nèg fè nèg. Bondye ri.
What man does to man makes God laugh.
People treat each other ridiculously.

Zepolèt pa zo saliè.
The shoulder decoration is not the shoulder bone.
One's honors are not one's true self.

Larivyè anpeche ou janbe men li pa anpeche ou tounen.
The river prevents you from crossing but it does not prevent
you from turning back.
You can always quit.

Yo fè pi bon wout ak yon vye baton.
One travels a better road with an old cane.
Experience helps.

Gason sansib pa jwen bon madanm.
The tender man doesn't find a good wife.
The nice guy doesn't win the girl.

Vòlè pa wont, men lafanmi wont.
The thief has no shame, but the family is ashamed.
A person's bad behavior brings shame to his family.

Lè m' kanpe, la wè longè m'.
When I stand up, he'll see my height.
I'll show him.

Twò konnen fè ou remèt rès.
Too much knowledge makes you give some back.
Knowing too much is sometimes uncomfortable.

Lè zombi goute sèl li pa mande rete.
When the zombie tastes of salt he doesn't want to stop. (It is
believed that salt can bring a zombie out of his trance.)
Awareness brings desire for more knowledge.

Twa fanm sifi pou fè yon mache.
Three women are enough to make a market.
A few women make a lot of talk.

Mamzèl konn lave kòb, li bwè dlo a.
The young lady knows how to wash money and drink the
water.
She knows how to get the most for her money.

Yo pa janm kenbe vòlè nan pye.
One never catches a thief by the foot.
*To be certain you need to catch a person red-handed, not with
circumstantial evidence.*

**Bouch granmoun santi tabak, men sa ki ladan l' se
pawòl.**
Old people's mouths stink of tobacco, but what's inside is
wisdom.
The old are full of wisdom.

Van woule pilon anndan kay fè nwa.
The wind blows the mortar (pestle) inside the darkened
house (even though it is heavy).
You have no idea what goes on behind closed doors.

Lè ou pèdi, ou peche.
When you lose, you sin.
No one likes a looser.

Lè timoun bezwen kriye, gade ou gade l', li kriye.
When a child wants to cry, just look at him and he cries.
A crybaby needs no encouragement.

Kote ki gen fanm fòk gen pale anpil.
Where there are women, there must be a lot of talk.
Women talk a lot when together.

Figi ou se paspò ou.
Your face is your passport.
A good reputation will take you anywhere.

Lè ou bezwen congo, ou rele l' yaya.
When you need the awkward person, you call him "yaya."
When you need someone, you get on his good side.

De chodyè gra anbarase yon chen mèg.
Two fat kettles confuse a skinny dog.
The situation is too much for him to handle.

De ti chen ap jwe; se youn ki pou tonbe.
Two puppies are playing; one must fall.
Two people are testing each other (bargaining), one must give in.

Malè yon nonm ki mete konfyans li nan yon nonm.
Woe to the man who puts his trust in another man.
All men are fallible.

Sa nou bezwen konnen, pouki sa kòk pa leve pye l' pou l' pise.
What we need to know is why the rooster doesn't lift its leg to piss.
Why is that person not behaving like others (as expected)?

Fanm se zanj; fanm se demon.
Woman is an angel; woman is a demon.
Women's emotions tend to be extreme.

Zantray fanm se rak bwa, yo bay tout kalite bèt.
Women's innards are a jungle, they give all kinds of beasts.
All kinds of people are born.

Fanm pa janm gen sekrè.
Women never have secrets.
Women tell each other everything.

Fanm se kajou. Plis li vye, plis li pi klere.
A woman is like mahogany. The older she gets, the more she glows.
She gets better with age.

Ou gen lajan ou gen fanm.
You have money you have women.
Women are attracted to wealth.

Fanm se kokoye, yo gen twa je yo wè nan youn.
Women are coconuts: they have three eyes, but they only see in one.
Women can be easily fooled.

Fanm, se asire pa sèten.
Women, it's sure they aren't certain.
Women are indecisive.

Nonm sa a, ou ka intelijan tankou l'; pase l', non.
You can be as intelligent as this man; more than him, no.
He's the smartest there is.

Ou fè timoun men ou pa fè santiman yo.
You make children, but you don't make their personalities.
You can't change who your children are at heart.

Fanm chanje menm jan ak tan.
Women change like the weather.
Women change their minds.

Van gen fòs sou tanga.
Wind has strength over an awning.
Persistence pays off. Nothing can resist the forces of nature.

Dèt gate zanmi.
Debt spoils friendships.
Lend money to a friend and he may become an enemy.

Pa marye pou lajan. Prete pi fasil.
Don't marry for money. Borrowing is easier.
Marrying for money doen't bring happiness.

Remèd pi rèd pase maladi.
Medicine is worse than sickness.
The cure is worse than the problem.

Jou ki ap vini pi long pase ane ke pase.
A day to come is longer than a year that's past.
Anticipation seems long.

Pa janm koupe dwèt moun kap ba ou manje.
Never cut off the finger of the one giving you food.
We must be grateful to the people who help us.

Pòch ki sonnen pa manke janmi.
A pocket that jingles lacks no friends.
When you have money you have friends.

Dlo sal refwadi fè cho.
Dirty water cools hot iron.
Gossip kills a friendship.

Pòch vid, kè lou.
Empty pockets, heavy heart.
Feeling sad without money.

Pa prese fè zanmi. Pa prese change zanmi.
Take your time to choose friends. Take your time to change friends.
Don't be to quick to make or to give up friendships.

San pa lave san.
Blood does not wash blood.
Two wrongs never make a right.

FATE, GOD AND THE SUPERNATURAL

Yon jou pou dyab, yon jou pou Bondye.
One day for the Devil, one day for God.

Se Bondye sèl ki konn doulè malere.
Only God knows the pain of the poor.

Yon jou pou dyab, yon jou pou Bondye.
One day for the Devil, one day for God.
Life is neither all good nor all bad. Evil and good both exist.

Jistis Bondye se kabouèt bèf.
God's justice is an oxcart.
God's judgment is slow but strong.

Mò pa konnen pri dra.
The dead don't know the price of sheets.
The dead don't care about funeral expenses. One must do whatever it takes to keep the spirits of one's ancestors happy.

Bèf san ke, Bondye pouse mouch pou li.
God shoos away the flies for the cow with no tail.
God takes care of those who cannot help themselves.

Pye joumou kouvri jaden men fòk li sèch.
The pumpkin vine covers the garden but it must dry up.
Everyone, including those who are very important, must die sooner or later.

Nèg fè lide l' jan Bondye ba l' dwa.
Man plans as God allows.
God is in control.

Lè poul bwè dlo, li pa bliye Bondye.
When the chicken drinks water, she doesn't forget God. (She raises her head to swallow.)
Remember to be thankful even in times of plenty. When you are vulnerable, you remember to rely on God.

Bèl antèman pa di paradi.
A beautiful funeral doesn't mean paradise.
Happiness is not determined by appearances.

Moso Bondye, moso slokoto.
A bit of God, a bit of the spirits.
Get help from both sides.

Yon moun pa janm mouri anvan lè l'.
A person never dies before his time.
All things in due time.

Move zèb ka leve toupatou.
Bad weeds can spring up everywhere.
Evil is everywhere.

Chans pa gen bonè.
Luck doesn't come early.
Good fortune is rare.

Bondye konn bay men li pa konn separe.
God gives, but He doesn't distribute.
Blessings are not distributed equally.

Chak kochon gen samdi pa l'.
Every pig has its Saturday.
Death comes to everyone. (Saturday is butchering day.)

Chak moun gen sò li.
Each person has a destiny.
Everyone is on earth for a reason.

Chak chaplè gen kwa pa li.
Each rosary has its own cross.
Every prayer is for a different purpose.

Chak jou, papye chanje nan biwo.
Every day, papers change at the office.
Each day brings changes.

Bondye pa bòpè, li se papa.
God is not a father-in-law; He's a father.
God's love is like that of a father to his son.

Se Bondye sèl ki konn doulè malere.
Only God knows the pain of the poor.
Only God cares about the poor.

Tout bagay se lòd.
Everything is ordered.
All things are predetermined.

Ou wè jodi a; ou pa konnen demen.
You see today; you don't know tomorrow.
The present is known; the future is not.

Tout moun konnen sa: le mal egzist.
Everyone knows this: evil exists.
Bad things happen.

Moun ki manke mouri dimanch se dimanch pou l' mouri.
He who almost died on Sunday will die on a Sunday.
What is meant to be will be.

Dye pa lòm.
God is not man.
Don't expect fate to be as you would have done things.

Bondye pa bay pitit li penn san sekou.
God never gives His children pain without help.
God will not test without giving His grace.

Kreyon Bondye pa gen gòm.
God's pencil has no eraser.
God does not change His mind.

Si Bondye voye ou, li peye frè ou.
If God sends you, He pays your expenses.
God will take care of you if you do His will.

Se Bondye ki pou ta Bondye vre.
It is truly God who would have to be God.
There is no one like God.

Lavi se yon machin san direksyon.
Life is an automobile without a steering wheel.
You can't control where life takes you.

Bondye konn kenbe krab mete nan makout avèg.
Sometimes God catches a crab and puts it in a blind man's sack.
God takes care of the needy.

Nan mal, nan mal nèt.
In evil, evil all the way.
Once a person begins doing bad things he rarely stops.

Ede tèt ou. Bondye va ede ou.
Help yourself; God will help you.
God helps those who help themselves.

M' pa pran Dye san konfès.
I don't take God without confession.
Reconciliation is reached through repentance. I don't expect something for nothing.

Bondye konnen pouki sa li bay chen maleng dèyè tèt li: pou l' pa ka niche l'.
God knows why He gives the dog a sore behind its head: so that it can't lick it.
God always has a purpose.

Se kaka rat ki nan ogatwa mwen ki fè m' deranje.
The rat turds in my offering box have me disturbed.
My good intentions were spoiled by someone else.

Lavi se yon boul; l'ap woule, ou pa konnen kote l'ap rete.
Life is a ball; it's rolling but you don't know where it will stop.
One doesn't know what life holds in store.

Kafou pi gran pase gran chemen.
A crossroad is greater than a wide road.
Having choices is good.

Mezi peche ou se mezi penitans ou.
The measure of your sin is the measure of your penitence.
The consequences equal the action. The punishment fits the crime.

Kabrit mouri kite mizè pou po li.
The goat dies and leaves misery for its skin.
Some problems survive a person.

Jou malè, ougan pa sèvi.
On the day of misfortune, the witchdoctor is of no use.
Fate cannot be resisted.

Je wouj pa boule kay.
Red eyes don't burn houses.
An evil look doesn't bring misfortune.

Dòmi pòv; leve rich.
Sleep poor; wake up rich.
Good fortune comes unexpectedly.

Ti Sonson fè lide l' men se Bondye ki ba l' dwa.
Little Sonson makes a plan, but God permits.
The ultimate decision lies in God's hands.

Nèg di san fè; Bondye fè san di.
Man talks without doing; God does without talking.
God does what He needs to do without a lot of fuss, but people often talk a lot with no action.

Lavalas pa janm bwote sa Bondye sere pou ou.
The torrent never carries away what God has in store for you.
God's will is forever.

Sa Bondye vle, se san repignans.
What God wants is without repulsion.
Accept fate.

Baryè ou rayi, se la solèy kouche ou.
The gate you hate is where the sun will set on you.
Fate will put you in the circumstance you least desire.

Lavi di ou, "Ann ale", men ou pa konnen ki kote l'ap mennen ou.
Life says, "Let's go," but you don't know where it is taking you.
You never know what the future holds.

Ou ka di konbyen ou genyen men ou pa ka di konbyen ou rete.
You can say how many (years) you have, but you can't say how many are left.
The past is known; the future is not.

Konprann se poul sou chay mwen ye.
Understand that I am a chicken on a market load.
I have no say. I'm just along for the ride.

Klòch Sentann di: "Ban m', m'a ba ou."
Saint Ann's bell says: "Give to me, I'll give to you."
The church promises blessings for offerings.

Jijman Bondye vini sou bourik.
The judgment of God comes on a donkey.
God's judgement is slow but steady and certain. God will reward the faithful.

Fòk ou mache pou ou wè kote lari a fè kwen.
You must walk to see where the street has corners.
One must live to see what life holds in store.

Ou konn sa ou kite; ou pa konn sa ou pral jwen.
You know what you left; you don't know what you'll find.
The past is known; the future is not.

Ki mele Bondye nan grangou chen.
What does God care about the dog's hunger?
God doesn't care about the problems of evil people.

Fòk gen maladi pou gen lanmò.
There must be sickness to have death.
Everything has a cause. There is more to the story than is known.

Bòkò di li rale moun nan bouch twou, men se Bondye ki fè gerizon.
The witchdoctor says he pulls people from the mouth of the grave, but it's God who does the healing.
God is in control.

Sa mwen wè pou ou, nèg nan Ginen pa wè l'.
What I see for you, those in Guinea don't see it.
I forsee the unpredictable coming to you (good or bad).

Lapenn pwofite.
Pain takes advantage.
Misfortune is compounded when things are bad. Things go from bad to worse.

Kòfrefò pa swiv kòbya.
The safe doesn't follow the hearse.
The dead don't take their possessions with them.

Lè sèt an ou echi, se ale pou ou ale.
When your seven years are up, you must go.
When your time is up, you must go.

Ale pou ou, tounen pou mwen.
Going is for you, returning for me.
My turn will come.

Ou bwè sa ou genyen; ou pa konn sa ou rete.
You drink what you have; you don't know what is left.
Live for today; you don't know the future.

DEALING WITH HARDSHIPS

Degaje pa peche.
Making do is no sin.

Chay soti sou tèt, tonbe sou zèpòl.
A load falls from the head onto the shoulder.

Degaje pa peche.
Making do is no sin.
Doing what one must to survive is not evil.

Chen achte tafya, chat bwe tafya, chen sou.
Dog buys rum, cat drinks rum, dog gets drunk.
You may not be at fault but you may still suffer the
consequences if you are involved.

Se pa tout twou ki gen krab.
Not every hole has a crab.
Disappointment. You can't always tell what will work out.

Chay soti sou tèt, tonbe sou zèpòl.
A load falls from the head onto the shoulder.
Things go from bad to worse.

Tete pa janm twò lou pou mèt li.
A breast is never too heavy for its owner.
One's own burdens will never be unbearable.

Se moun ki pran kou ki pare kou.
The one who has taken blows is the one who wards off
blows.
Those who have suffered are extra cautious.

Yon pye poul miyò pase yon bwa dan.
A chicken foot is better than a toothpick.
Receiving a little is better than nothing at all.

Bout kouto miyò pase zong.
A piece of a knife is better than a fingernail.
Something is better than nothing.

Bèl larivyè, nanpwen rad.
Beautiful river, no laundry.
One is unable to take advantage of a good situation.

Bitay fè ou vanse.
A stumble moves you forward.
We learn from our mistakes. A mistake is better than doing nothing.

Aprè lamès se vèp.
After the mass are vespers.
After joy is sadness.

Chat chode pè dlo frèt.
A scalded cat is afraid of cold water.
Those who have suffered are more cautious.

Koulèv mode l'. Li pè kòd.
Having been bitten by a snake he is afraid of a rope.
Those who have suffered are more cautious of repeating a mistake.

Pito lakwa ale kay zanmi; li pa ale lakay ou.
Better the cross go to your friend's house than to yours.
*Misfortune falling upon a friend is better than misfortune falling upon oneself. (Misfortune and difficulties are called a cross **Kalvè**/Calvary.)*

Depi nèg boule fòk li niche.
When one is burned, he must lick.
One must nurse a problem for as long as it exists.

Avan chwal te gen maleng, mouch te viv.
Before horses had sores, flies lived.
Freeloaders have always existed.

Dèyè se zèb; li taye; la pouse.
Behind is a weed; it is trimmed; it will grow.
Evil is punished, but it will always return.

Degoute mennen koule.
Dripping brings flowing.
Big things have small beginnings.

Pito ou wè lwen ou pa avèg.
Better to be farsighted than blind.
Something is better than nothing.

Pètèt pa asire.
Maybe is not sure.
Don't count on the unknown.

Pito dlo yanm grate ou, pase ou nan mizè.
Better the yam's sap itch you than you be in misery.
At least you have a yam to eat.

Chak pen gen founo li e fwomaj li.
Every bread has its oven as well as its cheese.
Everyone has trials and joys, and every trial has its joy.

Ti bouton mennen maleng; maleng mennen java.
Little pimples bring sores; sores bring ulcers.
Big problems have small beginnings.

Manje dan ou; di priyè ou.
Gnash your teeth; say your prayers.
You're out of luck.

Chak larivyè pote gravwa pa l'.
Every river carries its own gravel.
Every person has his/her own issues. Take care of your own problems.

Chik pa respekte granmoun.
Chiggers don't respect grownups.
Misfortune comes to all, including the rich and famous.

Genyen pa anpeche manke.
Having doesn't prevent lacking.
One always wants more than one has. One can always lose what one has.

Difisil pa bone; se la chans ki bay.
Difficulty is not a bonnet; it's luck that provides.
Be hopeful; something good may happen.

Egzile miyò pase fiziye.
Exile is better than being shot.
Living in an unfortunate situation is better than dying.

Kaka chen pa pikan men li fè ou bwete kan mènm.
Dog shit is not a thorn, but it makes you hobble nonetheless.
Some situations or people that don't hurt you are a nuisance nevertheless.

Tonbe ak roule nan falèz mare menm kote.
Falling and rolling over a cliff are tied in the same place.
Take care. The danger may be greater than you think.

Bondye di ou: fè pa ou, m'a fè pa m'.
God says to you, "Do your part; I'll do mine."
Do what you can and God will take care of the rest.

Lespwa fè viv.
Hope gives life.
Hope gives one the strength to carry on.

M' fin mouri, m' pa pè santi.
I'm already dead; I don't fear stinking.
I have nothing to lose.

Nan move pa, kabrit trenen bèf.
In a rough spot the goat drags the ox.
In tough times, the weak become strong.

Grangou dimanch pi rèd.
Hunger on Sunday is the toughest.
Your problems seem worse when you are not busy.

Mwen se bourik Senmak; tout kout pye bon pou mwen.
I am a donkey from Saint Marc; all kicks are good for me.
What you say and do can't hurt me.

Se chen m'ap leve pou m' kouche.
I'm moving dogs so that I can lie down.
I have nothing. I'm in bad shape.

Si bòt la twò jis pou ou, mache pye atè.
If the boot is too tight for you, walk barefoot.
Find a way to continue. Don't take on more than you can handle.

Si ane pa t' touye ou, jou pa ka touye ou.
If the year didn't kill you, the day can't kill you.
You have survived the worst of it, you can keep going.

Se lè van soufle ou wè dèyè poul.
It's when the wind blows that you see the chicken's behind.
When trouble stirs, true character is revealed.

Si ou pa lyon, fè ou rena.
If you aren't a lion, make yourself a fox.
If you aren't strong, be clever.

Nan mitan avèg, bòyn se wa.
In the midst of the blind, the one-eyed person is king.
Something is better than nothing.

Mizè pa konn doulè mèt li.
Misery knows not the pain of its owner.
Misery knows no mercy.

Maladi ranje doktè.
Sickness suits doctors.
Sickness makes business for doctors.

Bite pa tonbe.
Stumbling is not falling.
Correct your mistakes before it is too late. Hang in there.

Lajan pa fè moun, men lajan itil.
Money doesn't make a person, but money is useful.
Money is not everything, but it is important.

Kòl li se kòl swa; si ou mare l', la lage.
His necktie is a silk tie; if you tie it, it'll come loose.
He is impossbile to pin down.

Lamizè fè chwal angle pote makout sak pay.
Misery makes the English saddle horse carry straw bags.
When times are tough, even the rich must work.

Maladi antre sou chwal; li sòti sou bourik.
Sickness comes on a horse; it leaves on a donkey.
Sickness is quick to arrive and slow to leave.

Bab pi long, sousi pi vye.
The beard is longer; the worries are older.
Worries don't go away with time.

Kochon mawon konnen sou ki bwa pou l' fwote.
The wild pig knows on which tree to scratch itself.
A person in need knows who to turn to.

De moun mouye nan lapli, gen youn ki pi mal.
Two people get soaked in the rain; one is worse off.
There is always someone worse off.

Bout kouto miyò pase zong.
A piece of a knife is better than a fingernail.

Tout chay gen twòkèt li.
Every load has its pad.

Tout chay gen twòkèt li.
Every load has its pad.
Every problem has a solution.

Pito pitit kriye; manman pa kriye.
It is better for the child to cry than for the mother to cry.
Things are not as bad as they could be. (The mother cries if the child dies.)

Ti pil ti pil fè chay.
Little heap by little heap makes a load.
A lot of little problems lead to a heavy burden.

Lavi se kòd sapat; ou pa ka konte sou li.
Life is a sandal strap; you can't rely on it.
One never knows when life will let one down.

Ti kou ti kou bay fè mò.
Little blow by little blow brings death.
Problems add up. Persistence makes all the difference in solving a problem.

Lavi se yon pantalon defouke san bretèl.
Life is a pair of split pants without suspenders.
Problems all the way around.

Pito ou gen lajan; ou pa gen lespri.
Better to have money than intelligence.
Some ignorant people are rich, and some intelligent people are poor. Better to be rich.

Machwè brannen, grangou tchoule.
The jaw yawns like a horse, hunger backs off.
Distraction causes one to forget discomfort.

Mizè fè bourik kouri pase chwal.
Misery makes a donkey run faster than a horse.
Necessity makes a poor man work harder than a rich man.

Doktè pa chache malad, se malad ki chache doktè.
The doctor doesn't seek the sick; it is the sick that seek the doctor.
Those in need must take the first step.

Chen vòlè, men chen itil.
Dogs steal, but dogs are useful.
One has to tolerate inconveniences for certain benefits.

Moun ki ede ou achte chwal gwo vant pa ede ou ba l' manje nan sechrès.
The person who helps you buy a fat horse won't help you feed it during the dry season.
People who give you bad advice won't help you solve the resulting problems.

Bèf pa di savann mèsi.
The cow doesn't thank the pasture.
Being taken for granted.

Misye ap boukannen dlo.
The fellow is roasting water.
Desperation. Things are not going well.

Bèf la tombe mal; kòche l' mal.
The cow fell badly; butcher it badly.
Make the best of a bad situation.

Kabrit di: mwen manje zanmann men se pa bon li bon nan bouch mwen pou sa.
The goat says: I eat bitter almonds but that does not mean that they taste good.
I'm doing what I can, not what I wish.

Manje ou pa ka manje, se li ki donnen nan jaden ou.
The food you can't eat is the one that grows in your garden.
Your children will sometimes do what you would not do.

Lanmè pa kenbe kras.
The sea doesn't hold dirt.
Perspective. Troubles don't last.

Kabrit la pran fèy.
The goat takes leaves.
He does what he can. He does what is in his nature.

Chay pa janm lou pou mèt li.
The load is never heavy for its master.
You must be strong enough to carry your own problems.

Misye pran bal li ofon.
He took his bullet deeply.
He is suffering (emotionally) a great deal.

Moun ki bezwen deyò, chache chemen pòt.
The one who wants to leave seeks the way to the door.
You are free to leave.

Pòv pa mande degi.
The poor don't ask for extra.
Poverty makes you accept what you receive.

Je fon kriye devan.
The deepest eyes cry first.
Those with the most understanding hurt the most.

Chemen ou pa renmen, se ladan l' chwal ou toujou bouke.
The road you dislike is where your horse always tires.
The worst journeys seem to take the longest time.

Zèb ou pa vle nan jaden ou, se li ki pouse lakay ou.
The weed you don't want in your garden is the one that grows in your house.
Your children do wrong things you would not do.

Lè mayigwen mòde ou sou nen ou pa ka ba l' kou fò.
When a mosquito bites you on your nose you can't hit it very hard.
Deal with personal problems in a way not to cause yourself more trouble.

Malere pa nan bròdè.
The underprivileged don't show off.
Poverty makes one humble.

Dlo a tombe men kanari a la.
The water has spilled but the jug is safe.
The situation is not as bad as it could have been.

Plant ki plante nan bon dekou pa janm pèdi nèt.
A crop planted in a good season is never completely lost.
One who is properly raised will always find some measure of success.

Nanpwen renmen ki pa mande kite.
There is no love that doesn't ask to leave. There is no love that should not be left.
Every love has its hard times. Good fortune does not last forever.

Byen mal pa lanmò.
Very sick isn't death.
There's still hope.

Chemen bouton se chemen maleng.
The way to pimples is the way to sores.
One misery leads to another.

Nanpwen kavalie ki pa janm tonbe.
There's no horseman that never falls.
Everyone makes mistakes.

Zwazo joure men li pa joure pye bwa.
A bird may curse but not at a tree.
Don't criticize people you need.

Lavi se boukante mizè pou traka.
Life is an exchange of misery for problems.
Life is full of troubles.

Lè ou bezwen, ou dwe pi intèlijan.
When you are in need, you must be more intelligent.
Problems bring out creative solutions.

Kote ki gen dife a, gen dlo tou.
Where there's the fire, there's water, too.
Every problem has a solution.

Sa ou pa ta renmen wè nan latrin ou, ou wè l' nan lasal ou.
What you wouldn't want to see in your latrine, you see in your living room.
That which you most fear has happened. Family members cause the greatest hurts.

Ou kouche sou po bèf; ou pa vle pran odè li.
You sleep on the cowhide yet you don't want to smell it's odor.
You must take the bad with the good.

Dwèt ou santi, men ou pa ka koupe l' jete.
Your finger stinks, but you can't cut it off and throw it away.
A loved one has done something wrong but you cannot disown him/her.

Sa ki gen larivyè, twòp pou batwèl.
What is at the river is too much for the clothes paddle.
There are too many problems there for me to handle alone.

Sa nou bay pòv se Bondye nou prete l'.
What we give to the poor we lend to God.
A good deed never goes unblessed.

Kote chwal jete ou, la ou pase pye sou li ankò.
Where the horse throws you, there you throw your leg over it again.
Don't give up. Get right back on the horse.

Lè ou envite van vin lakay ou, ou bay bannann ou bwa.
When you invite the wind to your house, stake your banana plants.
Get ready for trouble.

Ou pa janm konnen kote dlo pase pou li antre nan bwa joumou.
You never know where water passes to enter into the pumpkin stem.
Mystery and persistence.

Gen anpil pa di kont, se pa gen ditou ki di kichòy.
Having a lot doesn't mean enough; it's not having anything that means something.
Don't be greedy; be thankful for what you have.

Lè w'ap neye, ou kenbe nenpòt branch ou jwen.
When you are drowning, you grab any branch you find.
In dire circumstances, one takes whatever help one can get.

Lè bab kamarad ou pran dife; mete pa ou alatranp.
When your buddy's beard catches fire; put yours to soak.
Learn from other people's mistakes.

Ou wè zwazo ap vole, men ou pa wè traka van ba li.
You see the bird flying, but you don't see the trouble the wind causes it.
We don't always recognize how hard other people work for what they have.

FOOD AND LIFE

Moun ki pa mange pou kò yo pa jamn grangou.
Those who don't eat alone are never hungry.

Lè ou soupe kay moun ou dòmi ta.
When you dine at someone's house, you sleep late.

Vant plen, dèyè sou.
Full belly, drunken backside.
You become lazy when you have eaten too much.

Bourik pa janm ranni devan zèb.
A donkey never brays in front of grass.
Food will keep people quiet.

Chen ki grangou pa jape.
The hungry dog doesn't bark.
One cannot work on an empty stomach.

Se foray ki kenbe bèf.
It's the hay that holds the cow.
Food keeps one close to home.

Sòt kou yon nonm sòt li konn lè l' grangou.
As stupid as a man may be, he knows when he's hungry.
Hunger is a feeling known to all.

Vant plen di "gwayav mi gen vè". Vant vid di "kite m' wè".
The full stomach says "the ripe guava has worms." The empty stomach says "let me see."
One is more picky about food when full than when hungry.

Nan tan grangou, patat pa gen po.
In times of hunger, the sweet potato has no skin.
When one is hungry, one isn't picky about food.

Kaka aran se vyann.
Herring dung is meat.
What one person rejects, another relishes. When in need, you eat what you find.

Bouch pa gou men anyen pa rete.
The mouth is not tasty, yet nothing remains.
You say that you don't care for it, but you ate everything.

Moun ki pa manje pou kò l' pa janm grangou.
Those who don't eat alone are never hungry.
Those who share will receive.

Lamizè fè chen monte kayimit.
Hunger makes a dog climb the star apple tree.
Need makes a person go to extremes.

Grangou nan vant pa dous.
Hunger in the stomach isn't sweet.
Hunger is misery.

Si kalmason te bon vyann, se pa nan mitan chemen yo ta jwen li.
If the slug were good meat, one wouldn't find it in the middle of the road.
Good food disappears quickly.

Kasav kanni bon lakay.
Mouldy cassava is good at home.
Even moldy bread tastes good when one is home.

Lamizè fè cheni manje fey tabak.
Misery makes the caterpillar eat tobacco leaves.
Hunger makes one desperate.

Moun grangou pa ka tande.
A hungry person can't hear.
Hunger makes one distracted.

Kote ki gen bouyon, gen soutni kè.
Where there is a broth, there is encouragement.
Food lifts the spirits.

Lestomak se kòf.
The stomach is a safe.
One cannot retrieve what one eats.

Sak vid pa kanpe.
An empty sack cannot stand.
Hunger makes one weak.

Granmoun pa ka mete rad ou, men yo ka manje manje ou.
The elderly can't wear your clothes, but they can eat your food.
One is never too old to eat.

Chen grangou pa kouche.
The hungry dog doesn't lie down.
Hunger makes one restless.

Jan pen ou ye, se konsa soup ou ye.
The way your bread is, that's how your soup is.
One compliments the other.

Lè ou grangou, gwayav pa gen vè.
When you're hungry the guava has no worms.
When hungry, one doesn't notice the imperfections in food.

Bwè tafya gen mèt li.
Drinking liquor has its master.
Some can handle alcohol and some cannot.

Nan manje apeti vini.
While eating, the appetite comes.
Knowledge leads to a desire for more.

Manje kwit pa gen mèt.
Cooked food has no owner.
Once cooked, food belongs to everyone.

Lè ou soupe kay moun ou dòmi ta.
When you dine at someone else's house, you go to bed late.
When someone is doing you a favor, you can't rush him.

Bouch pwason mete l' nan zen.
The fish's mouth gets him hooked.
One gets in trouble for what one says.

Se gou bouyon ki mete lang deyò.
It is the taste of the broth that brings out the tongue.
Good food leads to good conversation.

Bon nan bouch, boule vant.
Good in the mouth, burns the belly.
Not everything that looks attractive is good for you.
Consequences.

Lè chen ap bwè dlo, li di "se pa ou ki pa ou."
When the dog drinks water, he says, "It's yours that's yours."
Bad people don't share.

Si krapo te bon vyann, li pa ta mouri bò lanmè.
If the frog were good meat, it would not die on the seashore.
Not everything that looks edible is edible. Good food doesn't go to waste.

Se lakoujin ki di m' jan kay ye.
It's the kitchen that tells me how the house is.
The house is happy when there is food to eat.

Kote ki gen zo nanpwen dan.
Where there are bones, there are no teeth.
The one who has doesn't need, and the one who needs doesn't have.

GETTING BY

Kouri bourik ou, lale a gran.
Run your donkey; the road is wide.

Fòk ou antre nan dlo pou ou benyen.
You must get into the water to bathe.

Tanbou prete pa fè bon dans.
A borrowed drum doesn't make for good dancing.
Ownership provides the greatest satisfaction.

Kanpe sou bwa kwochi pou koupe yon bwa dwat.
Stand on a crooked branch to cut a straight pole.
Use what you have to get something better.

Bon mache koute chè.
Cheap is expensive.
You get what you pay for.

Se tè ki bat ki bwe lapli.
It's plowed earth that drinks the rain.
You must be prepared for opportunity.

De pye pa sonde larivyè.
Don't use two feet to see how deep a river is.
*Check things out carefully before committing everything to a
new venture.*

Bwè tafya; respekte boutèy.
Drink liquor; respect the bottle.
You have no use for that now but you will need it later.

Pa achte rad nwa nan nwit.
Don't buy black clothing at night.
Make sure you see and know what you are getting into.

Ti zwazo ki nan men plis pase zwa k'ap vole.
A little bird in the hand is worth more than a flying goose.
*The little something that's yours is more useful than the much
that does not belong to you.*

Piti piti zwazo fè nich.
Little by little the bird makes a nest.
Goals are accomplished one step at a time.

Pa pèdi yon founo pou yon sèl pen.
Don't lose an oven for a single loaf.
Don't lose everything while trying to save a part. Don't be greedy.

Pa bliye granchemen pou chemen dekoupe.
Don't forget the main road for the shortcut.
Keep on track. Keep your priorities.

Yon sèl dife pa kwit pwa.
One firing doesn't cook beans.
Some things take a long time to finish properly.

Tout bagay bon kay mèt yo.
All things are good at their owner's house.
People are proud of their own.

Pa koupe vant poul pou pran ze.
Don't cut open the chicken to take the egg.
If one ruins the source then there will be no more.

Kat je pa koupe bwa kwochi.
Four eyes don't cut a tree crookedly.
Working together gets the job done better.

Pye bèf pou pye bèf, mwen pito achte l' kay pratik.
One cow leg or another, I'd rather buy it at a favorite shop.
All things being equal, I'll stick with what I know.

Baton gonmye miyò pase de men vid.
A gum tree cane is better than two empty hands.
An inadequate tool or weapon is better than none.

Yon ze jodi pi bon pase yon poul demen.
An egg today is better than a chicken tomorrow.
You can count on what you have now more that what you may get later.

Fòk ou antre nan dlo pou ou benyen.
You must get into the water to bathe.
You must take risks if you want to accomplish something.

Panyòl pa kay.
A shed is not a house.
It is not what you would want but you must make do with what you have.

Bay bèf pou kabrit.
Give a cow for a goat.
A bad deal.

Moun swiv kouran.
People follow the current.
People do what they see others do.

Mwen pa't manje pwa, m' pa ka poupou pwa.
I didn't eat beans; I can't pass beans.
I can't give what I don't have. I can't confess to what I don't know.

Si ou kouvri dife, w'ap gen dife.
If you cover the fire, you will have fire.
Conservation now provides for later.

Bon pa gaspiye.
Good is not wasted.
Talented people are always needed.

Pito dlo a tonbe, kalbas la rete.
It's better that the water spills and the gourd remains.
It is better to lose the product than the source.

Pa kwoke makout ou pi wo pase men ou.
Don't hang your satchel higher than your hand.
Don't go beyond your means.

Se de bon ki fè bonbon.
It's two goods that make a "bonbon" (sweet).
To get along well everyone must be nice. This is a play on the Creole words good (bon) and sweets (bonbon).

Si ou gen baton, se pou chen pa mòde ou.
If you carry a stick it is so that dogs don't bite you.
A weapon should only be used for defense.

Nan goumen, grafonyen se kout zong.
In fighting, a scratch is a stroke of the fingernail.
Use what you have.

Pou fè kòb la fè mwa a, lave li, bwè dlo l'.
In order to make the money last the month, wash it and drink its water.
Stretch the money to make it last.

Fè koute chè.
Iron is expensive.
Quality is expensive.

Se sòt ki bay, enbesil ki pa pran.
It is stupid that gives and idiot that doesn't take.
Take what you are given.

Ou dwe pise pou pise.
You must piss to piss.
Take action. Don't just talk about it, do something.

Pati bonè pa di kont; se konnen wout la ki konte.
Starting early isn't enough; knowing the way is what counts.
Knowledge is better than eagerness.

Yon je pa je.
Eye is not eyes. (One eye is not a pair of eyes.)
More is better.

Pwomès se plezi moun sòt.
Promises please fools.
Don't be fooled by those who make big promises but never deliver Se pa chak jou Magarit al nan mache li fè bon konmisyion.

It's not every day Margarit goes to market that she does a good errand.
One must not expect the best every time.

Se ditou ki pa bon.
It's none that's bad.
A little of something is better than nothing.

Anpil ti patat fè chay.
Many little sweet potatoes make a load.
Many small things amount to much.

Rat anpil, twou pa fon.
Many rats, the hole isn't deep.
Too many people and not enough resources.

Longè bouji ou, longè priyè ou.
The length of your candle is the length of your prayer.
You only get what you pay for.

Mwend akasan plis siwo.
Less pudding; more syrup.
Please give me more of what I would rather have.

Se senk kòb ki fè goud.
Pennies make the gourd. (The gourd is the currency of Haiti.)
Little things can add up.

Kouri bourik ou, lale a gran.
Run your donkey; the road is wide.
Make the most of a good opportunity.

Dan se zo.
Teeth are bones.
When you master (chew) a subject the knowledge becomes useful.

Avantaj kòk se nan zepon l' li ye.
The rooster's advantage lies in his spurs.
Use your resources even if they are small.

Jako pa la nan lagè, men plim li ale.
The parrot doesn't go to war, but his feathers go.
Contribute what you can.

Moulen manje sou dan li genyen.
The mill grinds with the teeth it has.
Managing with what one has.

Pise krapo fè larivyè desann.
The frog's piss makes the river flood.
Even the smallest of actions can have big consequences.

Sa foumi genyen, se sa l' pòt nan mache.
The ant takes to market what she has.
A resourceful woman finds something to sell to earn money.

Kanari pa sous.
A jug is not a spring.
Just because there appears to be a lot of something does not mean that it will last forever.

Malfini manke poul; li pran pay.
The hawk missed the chicken and took the straw.
Escape from near disaster.

Mezi lajan ou, mezi wanga ou.
The measure of your money is the measure of your fetish.
You get what you can pay for.

Sa ki pa la, pa l' pa la.
The one who isn't here, his share isn't here.
To share the rewards, one must participate.

Pise mayengwen ogmante larivyè.
The mosquito's piss raises the river.
Even the tiniest of actions can have an effect.

Baton ou genyen se li ki pare kou pou ou.
The stick you have is the one that wards off blows for you.
Defend yourself with what you have.

Gadò pi fò pase mèt.
The shepherd knows more than the master.
Personal experience is worth more than academic teaching. A nanny has more influence over your children than you do.

Arenyen gen wit pat, si l' pèdi youn, sa pa anpeche l' mache.
The spider has eight legs, if it loses one, that doesn't prevent him from walking.
Keep a spare and use what you have.

Lè ou pa gen manman, ou tete grann.
When you don't have a mother you nurse your grandmother.
Make do with what you have.

Baton ou genyen se li ki "pinga chen ou."
The stick you have is your "stand off mutt."
Defend yourself with what you have.

Bwa ou pa bezwen, ou pa make l'.
The tree you don't need, you don't mark (claim) it.
Don't claim or take more than you need.

Dan ou genyen, se avè l' ou manje.
You eat with the teeth you have.
Make do with what you have.

Fanm gaspiyè toujou dwe.
The wasteful woman is always in debt.
Waste makes want.

Bwa move bwa men li bon nan dife.
The wood is bad wood, but it's good in the fire.
A rough person who is good in time of trouble. Everything has its use.

Dlo ki pou ou, se li ki tonbe nan ja ou.
The water that's yours is what falls into your jar.
Fate. What's yours is what comes to you.

Kote fil fini se la kouti fini.
Where the thread ends is where the sewing stops.
When the supply is gone, the work must stop. If you don't pay me, I won't keep working.

Gen kapab ak kapab; gen kapab pase kapab.
There's can and can; there's more can than can.
Both persons qualify but one is more capable.

Sa ki soti pa rantre.
What goes out doesn't return.
Be careful in spending money.

Lè kay ou piti, pran nat ou anba bra ou.
When your house is small, take up your mat under your arm.
Do what you have to, not what you wish, in order to get by.

Fò ou laboure ak bèf ou genyen.
You must plough with the cow you have.
Make do with what you have.

Sa ki pa sere pa ka chofe.
What is not left over can't be warmed up.
Don't waste; save some for later.

Sa ki nan men ou, se li ki pa ou.
What's in your hand is what's yours.
One can only count on what he owns. Don't make plans based on what is not certain.

Dlo ou piti; ou benyen akote.
Your water is little; you wash on the side.
Don't waste. Make do with what you have.

Ti bèf ou wete nan labou, se li ki bat ou.
The calf you pull from the mud is the one who fights you.
Ingratitude comes from those you help.

Kote ki gen chèn, nanpwen kou.
Where there is a necklace there's no neck.
The one who has doesn't need, and the one who needs doesn't have.

Ou pa bay chen an kanson; ou pa ka veye chita l'.
You didn't give the dog a pair of pants; you can't tell him how to sit.
Unless one provides the supplies, one can't dictate how they're used.

Se pa manke lang ki fè bèf pa pale.
It's not for the lack of a tongue that a cow doesn't speak.
Don't talk too much or repeat everything.

Ak po kò ou ou vini, ak po kò ou ou prale.
With your skin you came; with your skin you leave.
You can't take wealth with you when you die.

Aprann danse lakay.
Learn to dance at home.
Learn how to do a thing before you show others.

Traka pa avèti.
Trouble gives no warning.
Always be prepared.

Se grès kochon ki kwit kochon.
It's the fat of the pig that cooks the pig.
Profit keeps a business going.

WORK AND
EMPLOYMENT

Anpil men, chay pa lou.
With many hands a load is not heavy.

Se nan goute ou konnen gou rete.
It's by tasting that you know the aftertaste.

Bon kòk chante nan tout poulaye.
A good rooster crows in any chicken house.
A truly qualified leader is always prepared.

Jan ou bat tanbou a se konsa nou danse.
The way you beat the drum is the way we dance.
We're just following your orders.

Chak jou kiyè bwa al kay ganmèl men yon jou fòk ganmèl al kay kiyè bwa tou.
Every day the wooden spoon goes to the house of the wooden bowl but one day the wooden bowl must go to the house of the wooden spoon, too.
You must help those who work for you.

Li konnen manje farin, li pa konnen plante manyòk.
He knows how to eat flour, but he doesn't know how to plant casava.
He likes enjoying the benefits, but he doesn't like working.

Bon chwal toujou mouri ak maleng nan do.
A good horse always dies with sores on its back.
The best are overworked.

Mache chache pa janm dòmi san soupe.
Searching never sleeps without supper.
Effort pays off.

Fezè nat dòmi atè.
The mat maker sleeps on the floor.
A person who gets so caught up in providing for others that he forgets to provide for himself.

"Wi" pa monte mòn.
"Yes" doesn't climb the hill.
Talking doesn't get the job done. Agreeing doesn't guarantee follow through.

Kay kamarad pa nan mache.
A friend's house is not a market place.
Don't mix pleasure with business.

Yon sèl dwèt pa touye pou.
A single finger doesn't kill lice.
It takes teamwork.

Kapab pa soufri.
Can doesn't suffer.
A capable person will always find a way to earn a living.

Tout sa misye ap fè se dife pay.
All he is making is straw fire.
Futile labor soon lost.

Yon bourik aprann pi vit pase yon moun ki pa wè rezon pou l' aprann.
A donkey learns faster than a person who doesn't see any reason to learn.
Motivation is key.

Yon ti bout kòd rete vwayaj.
A little piece of rope holds up the journey.
Seemingly insignificant details can prevent success.

Moun pa konn achte chat nan makout.
A person doesn't buy a cat in a sack.
One must see what one is buying.

Toudi pa kwit chou.
Dizziness doesn't cook cabbage.
You are in no shape for that task. Beating around the bush doesn't get the job done.

Apre dans, tanbou toujou lou.
After the dance, the drum is always heavy.
After the party, clean-up is a chore.

Chanje mèt chanje metye.
Change masters; change trades.
You have a new master; you must work according to his taste.

Yon bon poul fè yon bon pitit; yon bon kòk fè yon bon ze pou fè yon bon pitit.
A good hen makes a good chick; a good cock makes a good egg to make a good chick.
Family background and upbringing both influence how a child turns out.

Tout myèl jalou pou siwo l'.
Every bee is jealous for her honey.
One is protective of one's possessions.

Tout voum se do.
Every load is a back.
All burdens must be carried.

Pito ou travay pase ou mande.
Better to work than to beg.
Any work is better than having to beg.

Chans pa vini de fwa.
Opportunity doesn't come twice.
You won't get another opportunity if you don't take this one now.

Kredi pa peye tèt li.
Credit doesn't pay for itself.
One is responsible for the payment of one's loans. Ventures taken on borrowed money will fail.

Pa bay bèf la babokèt lè l'ap rale kabouèt.
Don't muzzle the ox while he's pulling the cart. (Leave him unmuzzled so he can eat as he works.)
Don't be too controlling; allow people some freedom as long as they are getting the job done.

Devan grinbak, nanpwen fè back.
Faced with the greenback, there's no going back.
One will do anything for money.

Fasil kou bonjou.
As easy as good morning.
The simplest of tasks.

Tout boulin pa di kont se byen mache ki konte.
Running on all boilers (full speed ahead) isn't enough; it's running well that counts.
Working fast doesn't count unless the job is done right.

Lajan sere pa fè pitit.
Saved money doesn't make children.
Money doesn't increase unless it is put to work.

Prese bon; dousman bon.
Fast is good; slow is good.
There is a time to work and a time to rest.

Si ou pa gen lang, ou pa manje.
If you don't have a tongue, you don't eat.
You must say thank you for your food.

Byen san swe pa profite.
Possessions without sweat don't profit.
People do not appreciate things they have not earned.

"M'konnen fè" ak "m'a fè" se de.
"I know how to do" and "I'll do" are two (different things).
Knowledge does not constitute action.

Si se pa't koupe fè, machòket pa ta viv.
If it wasn't for cutting iron, the tinker wouldn't live.
A person with a difficult but necessary skill.

Piti piti, ti pay pay, zwazo fè nich.
Little by little, straw by straw, a bird makes her nest.
One step at a time.

Si ou chita, sa yo ba ou, se li pou ou vale.
If you sit then you must swallow what you are given.
If you don't participate in the work, you have no say in the rewards.

Nanpwen zamlèt san kase ze.
There is no omelet without breaking some eggs.
One must make necessary sacrifices to get a desired result.

Lajan se respè.
Money is respect.
Wealth brings status and respect.

Lajan se dyab.
Money is a devil.
Wealth brings out the worst in people.

Si ou manje lajan Shada, fòk ou peye l'.
If you eat Shada's money, you must pay for it.
You must work for your pay. Everything has a price.

Nan afè sa a, si ou pa pote w'ap trennen.
In this business, if you don't carry you'll drag.
You must do the work one way or another.

Si ou pa travay, wa fè lèd.
If you don't work, you'll act ugly.
Idleness brings trouble.

Se nan goute ou konnen gou rete.
It's by tasting that you know the aftertaste.
A person has the consequences of his/her actions.

Anpil men, chay pa lou.
Many hands, the load is not heavy.
Many helpers make a job easier.

Se konen ki fè, pa konen pa fè.
It's knowing that does, not knowing doesn't do.
One doesn't undertake a job one isn't qualified to do.

Se pozisyon ki fè aksyon.
It's position that takes action.
It takes qualification and opportunity both for good results.

Ti kochon, ti san.
Little pig, little blood.
Little capacity, little expectation.

Lajan fè chen danse.
Money makes a dog dance.
Money makes a person put on airs (pretense).

Machandiz ofri pa gen pri.
Merchandise offered has no price.
Everything is negotiable.

Lajan ra kou dan poul.
Money is as scarce as chicken teeth.
Money is hard to come by.

Lajan fè monte ma suife.
Money makes a person climb a greased flag pole.
Money makes one do extraordinary things.

Labou bouche kouran.
Mud clogs the flow.
A little hang-up can stop an entire project.

Machandiz ofri pa gen pri.
Merchandise offered has no price.

Chanje mèt chanje metye.
Change masters; change trades.

Responsab se chay.
Responsibility is a burden.
Responsibility is more trouble than glory.

Ranvwaye yon kaporal; pran yon sèjan.
Fire a corporal and hire a sergeant.
Get someone with more experience.

Avèg pa kondwi lapriyè.
The blind don't lead prayers. (They cannot see if eyes are closed.)
Not everyone is qualified for every job.

Kòmansman chante se soufle.
The beginning of singing is whistling. (Whistling leads to singing.)
One thing leads to another. There is more to come.

Yo pa chanje monti nan mitan pas dlo.
One doesn't change horses in the middle of a stream.
Get the job done now and take care of that later.

Moun sèvi ou, men yo pa chen ou pou sa.
People serve you, but they are not your dogs for that.
Treat employees with respect.

Afè leta pa janm piti.
State business is never small.
The state's dealings are never unimportant.

Yo pa kale kokoye pou po.
One doesn't shuck a coconut for its shell.
Futile labor.

Chita pa bay.
Sitting doesn't yield.
One must work to receive.

Sekwe tèt pa kase kou.
Nodding your head won't break your neck.
Saying yes won't hurt you.

Figi ki vann nan kredi se pa li ki ranmase kòb la.
The face that sells on credit is not the one that collects the debt.
One changes personalities when collecting a debt.

Ti koze menen gran zafè.
Small talk brings big deals.
Small leads to big (both good and bad).

Zwazo ki chante anpil pa gra.
The bird that sings a lot isn't fat.
Talk less and work more. Talking doesn't earn money.

Towo ki begle pa gra.
The bull that bellows is not fat.
More work, less talk. Talking doesn't earn money.

Chen ki gen bon dan pa jwen bon zo.
The dog that has good teeth doesn't find a good bone.
The one who is most qualified rarely gets the job.

Parese pa gen kay.
Laziness has no house.
No one admits to a job undone or poorly done.

Makak sou pa dwe tonbe devan pòt kay mèt li.
The drunken monkey shouldn't fall at his master's door.
Don't let your boss know of your foolishness.

Misye pa konn non chen li.
The fellow doesn't know the name of his dog.
He does not realize what kind of person he has working for him.

Sèvis prese, patat pa gen pò.
In a rush the sweet potato has no skin.
I'm in a hurry; give it to me as it is.

Premye so pa so.
The first fall is no fall.
The first failure is not defeat; keep trying.

Jaden lwen, gonbo di.
Far garden, tough okra.
That is a difficult job. The results may not be as you wish.

Intelijan twonpe leve bonè.
The intelligent fools the early riser.
Intelligence is more productive than hard work.

Chay ou pa ka pote, ou mete l' atè dousman.
The load you can't carry, you lay down gently.
Don't make excuses. Accept defeat graciously.

Plas leta se chwal papa.
A government position (job) is papa's horse.
A free ride.

Chemen long pa touye ou.
The long road doesn't kill you.
Perseverance is good.

Plis bourik la ka pote, plis yo chaje l'.
The more the donkey can carry, the more they load it.
More ability leads to more responsibility.

Chemen lajan pa gen pikan.
The path to money has no thorns.
One will endure anything for money.

Bourik chaje pa kanpe.
A loaded donkey doesn't stand still.
No rest for the busy.

Sa n'ap fè, se li n'ap okipe.
What we're doing is what we're taking care of.
We are taking care of business.

Ouvriye vann zouti li men li pa vann metye li.
A worker sells his tools, but he doesn't sell his trade.
A man sells his labor but not himself. A man's profession can never be taken from him.

Nanpwen mòn ki pa gen chemen dekoupe.
There is no mountain that doesn't have a shortcut.
There is always an easier way.

Lapli te tonbe pase sa. Tè te bwè l'.
The rain fell more than that. The ground drank it up.
Too much talk. That idea has already been tried and failed.

Rat ki gen yon sèl twou mouri fasil.
The rat that has only one hole dies easily.
If you have only one trade, you may starve.

Koulèv ki konn lajè gòj li, se li ki vale krapo.
The snake that knows the width of his throat is the one that swallows frogs.
A man who knows his abilities doesn't take on more than he can handle.

Jan chat mache, se pa konsa li kenbe rat.
The way a cat walks is not how it catches rats.
Each task has its own requirements.

Sèpantye fouye twou, zandolit kouche ladan l'.
The woodpecker drills a hole and the lizard sleeps in it.
One man profits from another man's efforts.

Dwèt pa janm di gade m'. Li di gade la.
A finger never says look at me. It says look there.
The guilty always point at others.

Toujou gen retay kay tayè.
There are always scraps at the tailor's house.
One's profession leaves its mark. Some things go together.

Nanpwen metye ki pa nouri mèt li.
There's no trade that doesn't feed its master.
Any honest work is good work.

Chen bwè dlo la rivyè men li pa sal li pou sa.
The dog drinks from the river but that doesn't meant that it doesn't dirties it.
A good reputation survives lies and criticism.

W'ap pase monte, ou pa wè m'; lè w'ap pase desann w'a wè m'.
You don't see me on your way up, but you'll see me on your way down.
You ignore me when you are doing well, but you come to me when you need me.

Chen pa manje bannan, men li pa vle poul beke l'.
A dog doesn't eat plaintains (bananas), but he doesn't want a chicken to peck at them.
A bad person doesn't want others to benefit even when it costs him nothing.

Twòp grate kreve kwi.
Too much scrubbing wears a hole in the wooden bowl.
Too much work wears one out.

Se de dwèt ki touye pou.
It takes two fingers to kill lice.
Working together solves the problem.

Mache pou anyen, chita pou anyen, mwen pito chita.
Walking for nothing, sitting for nothing, I would rather sit.
I'd rather not waste my energy.

Kote bèf la mare, se la pou l' manje.
The ox must eat where it is tied.
An employer must take care of his employees.

Sa ou wè se twòkèt; chay la dèyè.
What you see is the padding; the load is yet to come.
The real challenge is yet to come.

Lè chen pa vle kenbe kabrit, li di pye l' fè l' mal.
When the dog doesn't want to catch a goat, it says its feet hurt.
One makes excuses to get out of working.

Mache twonpe chita.
Walking fools sitting.
Keep busy and you will forget about your problems.

Pise gaye pa kimen.
Spread piss doesn't foam.
A person who spreads his time between too many projects doesn't do any of them well.

Douz metye, trèz mizè.
Twelve trades, thirteen miseries.
Too much training, not enough working.

Ou fin vann, ou fin achte.
When your selling is finished your buying is over.
If you have nothing to sell you can't afford to buy anything. One must work to afford to live.

Lè ou pran asosye, ou pran yon mèt.
When you take a partner, you take a master.
With a partner you are not free to do as you wish.

Virtues and Vices

Sòt pa touye, men li fè ou swe.
Stupid doesn't kill you, but it makes you sweat.

"Pito sa" pase "malgre sa".
"Better this" than "in spite of this."

Di m' ki sa ou renmen, m'a di ou ki moun ou ye.
Tell me what you love, and I'll tell you who you are.
Your priorities shape your character.

Pale verite men pati la menm.
Speak the truth, but leave right away.
It is best to wait until leaving to be honest.

Kay koule twonpe solèy, men li pa twonpe lapli.
A leaky roof fools the sun but it doesn't fool the rain.
One's faults will be exposed sooner or later.

Se "si m' te konnen" ki toujou koupab.
"If I had known" is always guilty.
Ignorance is a convenient excuse.

"Pito sa" pase "malgre sa".
"Better this" than "in spite of this."
Optimism surpasses pessimism.

Bay manti pou sove yon nonm, men pa pou mete l' nan prison.
Lie to save a man but not to put him in jail.
Lying is all right if it's for a good cause.

Pwomès se dèt
Promise is a debt.
One is bound to a promise.

Rann sèvis tounen chagren.
Rendering service turns to grief.
Doing a favor for others often causes problems.

Charite pa gen gou.
Charity has no taste (preference).
Those who beg cannot choose what they get.

Abitid se vis.
Habit is a vice.
Habits are difficult to break.

Move manyè, twa pa devan kakalanga.
Bad manners are just three steps ahead of the "gobble-gobble" (turkey).
Bad manners lead to worse ways.

"Anvi wè" monte kay li bò gran chemen.
"Eager-to-see" builds his house along the highway.
Curiosity.

Granmèsi chen, se kout baton.
A dog's thanks is a beating.
Ingratitude.

Bato koule pa anpeche lòt navige.
A sunken ship doesn't prevent others from sailing.
Others' failures do not inhibit one's success.

"Men non" se lizaj. "Non mèsi" se delivrans.
"Not at all" is common. "No thank you" is a relief.
Manners are appreciated.

Nèg sòt se manje boule.
A stupid man is burned food.
A person who does not measure up to his potential.

Chen pa janm twò vye pou l' anraje.
A dog is never too old to go mad.
It's never too late for someone to turn against you.

Fanm jalou pa janm gra.
A jealous woman is never fat.
Jealousy causes one to be sick with worry.

Dèyè do se nan Ginen.
Behind the back is Guinea.
Mistrust comes from betrayal and slavery.

Lalin kouri jouk li jou.
The moon runs until it is day.
Evil deeds can be hidden for a while, but the truth will eventually be exposed.

Ipokrit se kouto de bò.
A hypocrite is a double-edged knife.
A hypocrite has two faces. He is dangerous.

Zwazo ki gen anpil plim pa chante.
Birds with many feathers don't sing.
People who have a lot of possessions should not brag and draw attention to themselves.

Granmèsi zoranj se kout gòl.
An orange's thanks is a blow of the pole.
Ingratitude.

Responsab pa gen gwo vant.
A person with responsibilities doesn't have a big belly.
A person who must take care of others has no time for himself.

W' ap fè la fou pou pa peye dwa.
You're acting crazy to avoid paying taxes.
Putting on an act to avoid consequences. It is costing you more to avoid doing something you don't want to do.

Kalkile pa gra.
Worry is not fat.
Worrying is unhealthy.

Fou devan; dèyè pa konnen.
The craziness up front, behind doesn't know.
Two-faced.

Piti pa chich.
A little is not stingy.
Even small gifts should be appreciated.

Yon moun ki konn danse, se nan fent ou pran l'.
It takes trickery to catch a person who knows how to dance.
You must be smart to catch or work with a clever person.

Pa okipe misye, kochon manje santiman l' nan po bannann.
Pay no attention to this man; pigs have eaten his feelings on a banana skin.
He has no conscience.

Chita chita kanson fini.
Sitting and sitting wears out the pants.
Lazy people use up resources without getting anything done.

Se malonnèt ki mennen repwòch.
Dishonesty brings reproach.
You will be criticized for wrongdoing.

Tout maladi pa maladi doktè.
Not every illness is a doctor's illness.
Some illnesses have unknown causes (spirits).

Chak moun gen yon gren zanno kay ofèv.
Everyone has an earring at the jeweler's.
No one is perfect.

Byen vini pa konn ansyènte.
Doing well knows not the past.
In one's prime and not appreciating traditions.

Moun afre wont.
Greedy people are ashamed.
Greed brings shame.

Vòlè vòlè vòlè, dyab ri.
Robber robs robber; the Devil laughs.
The joke's on you.

Li remèt li yon sigarèt limen nan de bout.
He gave him a cigarette lit at both ends.
He got him into trouble.

Chich kouwè kayimit.
Stingy as a star apple.
The stingiest of stingy. (The fruit of the star apple tree never falls, not even when ripe. It must be plucked.)

Pran kòlè sèvi wont.
Using anger for shame.
The guilty use anger as a defense.

Vye chodyè kwit bon manje.
An old pot cooks good food.
The elderly are full of wisdom.

Si pa gen sitirè, pa gen vòlè.
Without tolerance there are no thieves.
Soft on crime breeds crime.

Si ou bwè se pou ou sou.
If you drink, you must get drunk.
Count on the consequences of your actions.

Ann afè pa dòmi.
In business doesn't sleep.
Work and responsibilities keep one from being idle.

Li pa janm twò ta pou chat soupe.
It is never too late for a cat to eat supper.
Some people never miss an opportunity to take advantage.

Si ou pa bouke, w'a mantò.
If you aren't tired, you'll lie.
Idleness brings trouble.

Nan ede pote, ou ka tounen bèt chay.
In helping to carry, you may turn into a pack animal.
Give a hand, but don't be taken advantage of.

Mwen voye dlo, men mwen pa mouye pèsonn.
I throw water, but I don't get anyone wet.
I'm complaining, but I'm not hurting anyone.

Bwa a pa bon nan dife, men li fè lafimen.
It is not good firewood but it makes smoke.
A troublemaker who is not productive.

Anba levit fè nwa.
It's dark under the jacket.
One doesn't know what another person may be hiding.

Se bon ki ra.
It's good that's rare.
A good thing is hard to find.

Se bon kè krab ki fè l' san tèt.
It's the crab's big heart that makes it not have a head.
A person who is kind but not always wise.

Fòse je pase nwit.
Force the eyes to pass the night.
Asking something difficult. Worry.

Sèl vòlè bèf ki vòlè.
Only a cow thief is a thief.
A small theft is no crime.

Moun onèt antre toupatou.
Honest people enter everywhere.

Abitid se vis.
Habit is a vice.

Lanmou se plezi; lonè se devwa.
Love is pleasure; honor is duty.
The duty to one's honor surpasses love.

Lajan kase wòch.
Money breaks rocks.
People will do anything for money.

Logèy degrese lòm.
Pride thins a man.
A prideful person loses respect.

Labou rete kouran.
Mud stops the creek.
Evil sometimes prevents good.

Kochon pa janm fache ak labou.
Pigs don't get angry at mud.
Bad people like bad things.

Lotri se baton avèg.
Lottery is the blind man's cane.
The foolish rely on chance.

Mete pye sou chen; wa konnen si l' konn mòde.
Step on a dog and you'll know if it bites.
An evil person will hurt you if you get in his way.

Pi gran nèg se moun ki fè respè l'.
The greatest person is the one who respects himself
(behaves as he should).
Honor comes in doing what is right.

Wont pi lou pase sak sèl.
Shame is heavier than a sack of salt.
Shame is hard to bear.

Chat konnen, rat konnen; barik mayi a rete kanpe.
The cat knows, the rat knows; the barrel of corn stands.
It is impossible to be dishonest when everyone knows the truth.

Dan ri malè.
Teeth laugh at misfortune.
You laugh when you should cry.

Chen vòlè tabak menm si l' pa fimen.
The dog steals tobacco even if he doesn't smoke.
A thief is indiscriminate.

Lanmò bourik ranje chen.
The donkey's death suits the dog.
Evil people take advantage of others' misfortunes.

Mouch pa bezwen vyann nan, men li gate l'.
The fly doesn't need the meat, but it spoils it.
Moochers waste what's not theirs.

Tizon dife di li fou, men li pa janm pran chemen larivyè.
The fire spark claims to be crazy, but it never takes the path to the river.
A sly person.

Sòt pa touye, men li fè ou swe.
Stupid doesn't kill you, but it makes you sweat.
When you don't do something right the first time you will have to do it again.

Nèg sòt monte chwal li devan dèyè.
The foolish person rides a horse backwards.
The foolish do things all wrong.

Krapo fè kòlè, li mouri san dèyè.
The frog gets angry; it dies without its behind.
Anger will do one in.

Koukou chante non li.
The cuckoo bird sings his name.
The stupid sing their own praises.

Pati bonè pa di konn chemen pou sa.
Starting early doesn't mean knowing the way.
Eagerness doesn't insure competence.

Labonte krapo fè l' mouri san dèyè.
The frog's goodness makes it die without its behind.
One's goodness will do one in.

Gran banda zandolit fè l' mouri inosan.
The lizard's cockiness makes him die innocently.
Pride makes people do foolish things.

Nèg sòt bouyi aran sèl; li mete sèl ladan l'.
The stupid man boils salted herring and puts salt on it.
A stupid person tends to overdo things.

Gason kou rèd konte kòb nan pòch.
A man with a stiff neck counts his change in his pocket.
A stingy person keeps his money hidden.

Nèg sòt se chwal move zespri.
The stupid man is the horse of the evil spirit.
Stupidity facilitates evil.

Bourik te mèt abiye kon l' abiye, kou l' midi, fòk li ranni.
The donkey may be as dressed up as he can be, but as soon as it is noon he must bray.
Don't be fooled by looks; sooner or later, one's true nature will come out.

Kochon wonfle, se pa pou sa li dòmi.
The pig snores, but that doesn't mean he sleeps.
Don't be fooled by what that person is saying.

Moun onèt antre toupatou.
Honest people enter everywhere.
There's no reason to fear an honest person.

Po kabrit pa ase pou kouvri tanbou, Bouki ap mande moso pou l' boukannen.
The goat's skin isn't enough to cover a drum; Bouki is asking for a piece to roast.
The foolish ask for more when there isn't enough to go around.

Nèg sòt mare chwal li. Nèg lespri pa ka lage l'.
The stupid person ties his horse. The wise man cannot loosen it.
Street smarts go a long way.

Vòlè pa janm renmen vòlè parèy li.
A thief never likes other thieves.
One who is dishonest distrusts others.

Nonm sa a mouri, se santi, li poko santi.
This man is dead; he just has not begun to stink.
He has already lost the battle but has not yet given up.

Vòlè pa janm vle kamarad li pote yon gwo makout.
A thief never wants his friend to carry a big sack.
Those who are guilty don't trust others.

Pi rèd pase kouto de bò.
Worse than a two edged knife.
Two-faced.

Voye wòch; kache men.
Throw rocks; hide the hand.
A hypocrite or gossiper.

De zòm onèt vann chwal yo san lavant.
Two honest men trade a horse without a receipt.
An honest person's word can be trusted.

Rebouè se nòs.
To drink again is a wedding.
Only indulge on special occasions.

Atansyon, misye se chen ki mòde an trèt.
Watch out; he is a dog that bites on the sly.
He is sly and dishonest.

San rekonezans reveye repwòch.
Ungratefulness awakens reproach.
Ungrateful people bring reproach upon themselves.

Twòp bwòdè fè krab pèdi twou l'.
Too much strutting makes the crab lose its hole.
Pride goes before the fall.

Ki mele pis ak grangou chen?
What does the flea care about the dog's hunger?
Moochers don't care about those they use.

Lè ou manje pitit tig, ou pa dòmi di.
When you eat the tiger's cub, you don't sleep tight.
The guilty can't relax for fear of retribution.

Lè ou krache anlè, li tonbe sou pwent nen ou.
When you spit into the air, it falls on the tip of your nose.
Cockiness will backfire.

Pa dekouvri Senpòl pou ou kouvri Senpyè.
Don't uncover Saint Paul to cover Saint Peter.
Never borrow from one person to pay another.

Timoun chich kriye de fwa.
The selfish child cries twice.
A greedy child cries from wanting and again from the consequences.

Sou pa manti.
Drunk doesn't lie.
When under the influence of alcohol, people tend to tell the truth.

Pa pale zòrèy mal devan bourik.
Don't speak badly of ears in front of a donkey.
Don't criticize faults that apply to those present.

Kote ki gen chawony se la ki gen chen.
Where there is garbage is where the dogs will be.
Bad people gather in bad places.

Ou vle tout ou pèdi tout.
You want all; you lose all.
Greed causes loss.

Mantè bliye.
Liars forget.
A dishonest person forgets and is inconsistent.

Pa mare bourik ki pa pou ou.
Don't tie a donkey that is not for you.
Mind your own business.

Tout bèt nan lanmè manje moun, men se reken ki pote move non.
Every animal in the sea eats people, but it's the shark that has a bad name.
One person bears the bad reputation for another's actions.

Ou se poul kay, mwen pa bezwen mayi pou m' kenbe ou.
You're a household chicken; I don't need corn to catch you.
You are easy to fool.

SOCIAL COMPARISONS

Ti nèg fè sa l' kapab. Gran nèg fè sa l' vle.
The little guy does what he can.
The big shot does what he wants to.

Nan mitan diri, ti wòch goute grès.
In the rice, a pebble tastes the fat.

Wòch nan dlo pa konnen doulè wòch nan solèy.
The stone in the stream knows not the pain of the stone in
the sun.
Those with an easy life don't care about the suffering of others.

Bourik pa'p travay pou chwal galonnen.
A donkey won't work for the horse to gallivant.
*Workers will rebel under a frivolous boss. It is unfair for the poor
to work so that the wealthy can benefit.*

Malere pa dezonè.
Poverty is no dishonor.
It is no shame to be poor.

Tout vye vis se pou malere.
All vices are for the poor.
*When anything wrong is done, a poor person always gets the
blame.*

Pye kout pran devan.
The short foot takes the lead.
*Those who are less capable need those who are more competent
to look over their shoulders.*

Gwo non touye ti chen.
A big name kills the puppy.
Too much power too young proves fatal.

Poul kouve ze kanna men li pa benyen nan larivyè ak li.
A chicken will sit on a duck's eggs but won't swim in the
river with it.
*A person will do some things for another but cannot do
everything.*

Pale franse pa di lespri.
Speaking French doesn't mean intelligence.
Putting on airs does not make one intelligent.

Manje kay moun pa janm plen vant ou.
Eating at someone else's house never fills your stomach.
You will never be satisfied when someone else is in charge.

Gran kay pran dife, ki dire la koujin.
Great houses catch fire not to mention the cookshack.
If the great are succeptible to harm all the more so are the weak.

Bèl cheve pa lajan.
Beautiful hair is not money.
Beauty doesn't make one wealthy.

Tout bwa se bwa men mapou pa kajou.
All wood is wood, but the mapou tree isn't mahogany.
All people are people, but they're not all the same.

Rad pa janm fè moun.
Clothes never make the person.
Identity lies within. You cannot hide what kind of person you really are.

Si bèf te konn fòs yo, majoral pa ta lanse yo.
If cows knew their strength, they would not be butchered.
You are stronger than you realize. You have more power than you have been led to believe.

Pi wo pran pi gwo so.
Greater takes a bigger fall.
The greater one is, the more there is to lose.

Depi ou pran ka piskèt, fòk li mande kokoye.
As soon as you take up the case of the small fry, he must ask for a coconut. (Coconuts are difficult to pick.)
Grant an unimportant person a request and he will ask for the impossible.

Se sou bwa ki gen fwi yo voye wòch.
It's at the branch that has fruit that rocks are thrown.
Only those who have are robbed.

Depi sou kòlèt ou mwen wè rejiman ou.
From your collar I see your regiment.
It's very obvious what kind of person you are.

Kondane malfini; kondane manman poul tou.
Condemn the hawk; condemn the hen, too.
Don't show favoritism.

Bourik rete bourik, menm lè l' gen sèl sou do l'.
A donkey remains a donkey, even when it has a saddle on its back.
Putting on airs doesn't change a person's abilities.

Pòt tè pa goumen ak pòt fè.
A clay pot doesn't fight with an iron pot.
The weak can't fight the strong.

Pyan pa respekte bounda gran mouche.
Yaws doesn't respect the rich man's behind.
Misfortune comes to the wealthy as well as to the poor. When it comes to the bottom of things, we're all the same.

Se lavil bonbon soti monte nan mòn.
It's from town that sweets go up to the mountains.
The best is from the city. The poor benefit from the wealthy.

Menm lè li pote relik, bourik toujou bourik.
Even if it carries a religious artifact, the donkey is still a donkey.
Putting on airs doesn't change a person's status.

Fiyèl mouri; kòmè kaba.
Godchild dies; godmother is finished.
Get rid of the subordinates and the leaders will fall.

Se sou chemiz blanch yo wè tach.
It's on the white shirt that a stain is seen.
Those of the best reputation are the most susceptible to scandal.

Se toujou sou chen mèg yo wè pis.
It's always on the lean dog they see fleas.
The poor get away with nothing.

Ayiti dwe lafrans.
Haiti owes France. (Haiti was a French colony.)
We are indebted to our elders, even those we did not like.

Dlo manyòk pa lèt.
Cassava water isn't milk.
Two things may look alike, but that doesn't make them the same.

Li pa ka fè ka l' si l' se chen.
He can't make his case if he is a dog.
It is difficult for a person with a bad reputation to convince others of his innocence.

Mwen byen sangle; m' pa foule.
I'm well girthed; I won't be sprained.
I'm well connected; I won't be harmed.

Si reken di ou pwason avèg, se pou ou kwè l'.
If a shark tells you that fish are blind, believe him.
Don't argue with those more powerful than yourself.

Se piti ki mennen gwo.
The small lead the big.
The wealthy rely on the poor.

Ti klòch, gwo son.
Little bell, big sound.
The less capable often talk the most.

Ti pwason fri vit.
Little fish fry quickly.
The little guy is the first to go.

Chare chen pa mal, se tranble janm lan ki rèd.
It's not hard to imitate a dog, it's the twitching of the leg
that's tough.
One can only go so far in pretending.

Maladi gate vanyan.
Disease spoils the fit.
Everyone gets sick.

Lè poul mare, ravèt fè l' eksplikasyon.
When the chicken is tied the cockroach lectures her.
The weak feel powerful when the strong are helpless.

Se lè ou genyen, zanmi konnen ou.
It's when you have that your friends know you.
Wealth brings friends.

Nesesite pa konnen bon ras.
Need doesn't know good race (family).
Misfortune can come to anyone.

Lajan al kay lajan.
Money goes to the house of money.
The wealthy get wealthier.

Ti kwi antoure ja.
Little dippers surround the jar.
The big shot is surrounded by helpers.

Lajan gen odè.
Money has an odor.
Money is not clean. Wealth has a price.

Nan mitan diri, ti wòch goute grès.
In the rice, a pebble tastes the fat.
Because of a wealthy friend a poor man tastes the good life.

Abitan pa janm konnen.
Peasants never know.
No value is given to the opinions of the poor.

Se piti m' piti; men mwen pa pitimi san gadò.
Little though I'm little, I'm not millet without a guardian.
I have my protectors.

Piti kou l' piti, lanmori se vyann.
Little as it may be, dried cod is meat.
The little guy is somebody, too.

Fèy mapou sanble ak fèy manyòk.
Mapou tree leaves look like manioc leaves.
The powerful and the weak have many things in common.

Lajan pa fè boul monnen nan pòch malere.
Money doesn't pile up in the poor man's pocket.
The poor spend what money they have.

Lajan fè lòm.
Money makes a man.
Money gives one status.

Pa janm bay chen kanson.
Never give pants to dogs.
Don't make someone out to be more than he is.

Sou bèk fesi ou, yo wè nan ki rejiman ou ye.
On your cap bill, they see what regiment you are in.
It's easy to see what kind of a person you are.

Santi bon koute chè.
Smelling good costs a lot.
Popularity has a price.

Dan pouri gen fòs sou bannann mi.
Rotten teeth have strength over ripe bananas.
Even the weak have their strengths.

Ray pou ray; tren pou tren.
Rail for rail; train for train.
Stick with your own kind/class.

Prizon fèt pou tout moun.
Prison is made for everyone.
The law applies to all.

Pale Franse pa fè m' pè.
Speaking French doesn't scare me.
You don't impress me with your airs.

Poul pa chante devan kòk.
The chicken doesn't crow in front of the rooster.
Don't show off in front of the boss.

Si bonbòn poko plen boutèy pa ka jwen.
If the jug isn't full the bottle cannot have any.
The big man gets his fill before the little man is served.

Ti poul pa mande plim; li mande lavi.
The baby chick doesn't ask for feathers; it asks for life.
A poor man doesn't want much.

Pale Fransè pa voye nan mache.
Speaking French doesn't send to the market.
Fancy ways don't get the job done.

Lawouze fè banda tout tan solèy poko leve.
The dew puts on a show until the sun comes up.
The little guy shows off when the big shot is not around.

Zafè gran nèg se mistè.
The affairs of a big shot are mysteries.
The powerful keep their business a secret.

Nèg pa fye nèg depi nan Ginen.
People don't trust each other since Guinea.
The distrust between people often has deep roots. (In Guinea, slaves' ancestors sold each other into slavery.)

Dan pa janm gen rezon devan jansiv.
Teeth are never right before the gums.
Those who do the work are never right to those who benefit.

Gwo chen tonbe, ti chen tonbe.
The big dog falls, the little dog falls.
When the big shot goes down, so does the little man.

Gran nèg antre kote l' vle.
The big shot enters where he wants.
Power gives one the privilege of choice.

Gran nèg se leta.
The big shot is a state.
Those with power call the shots.

Kaptèn zombi se yon nonm tou.
The captain of the zombie is a man, too.
Even the most powerful are only human.

Kòk twò fen pa al nan batay.
The cock that's too fine doesn't go into battle.
An educated fancy person who is impractical.

Lè chat pa la, rat bay kalenda.
When the cat is gone, the rats throw a kalenda ball.
When the boss is not present, the workers are free to celebate.
(The kalenda was a forbiden dance slaves held in secret).

Tanbou rete danse.
The drum stops the dancing.
The leader calls the shots.

Kòk ki gen pye sal, se sou do poul li souye l'.
The rooster with dirty feet wipes them on the chicken's back.
Men abuse women.

Bourik travay, chwal galonnen.
The donkey works; the horse gallivants.
The little man must work while the big shot enjoys life.

Moun mouri pa konn valè dra blan.
The dead don't know the value of a white sheet.
Luxury doesn't matter to those who can't enjoy it.

La wouze di li bèzò, se tout tan solèy pa leve.
The dew says he is hot stuff so long as the sun is not up.
The little guy is free to brag until the big shot appears.

Mapou tonbe, kabrit manje fèy li.
The mapou trees falls; goats eat its leaves.
The mighty fall and others benefit.

Chen ki gen zo nan bouch li pa gen zanmi.
The dog that has a bone in his mouth has no friends.
A rich man has no friends.

Manjè ze pa konn doulè manman poul.
He who eats eggs knows not the pain of the hen.
Those who reap the benefits don't appreciate the labor of the workers.

De mèg pa fri.
Two leans don't fry.
One poor person doesn't have enough to help another.

Devan pòt tounen dèyè kay.
The front door becomes the back of the house.
Things change. Situations may become reversed.

Je ki pa wè sousi di la kòmande.
The eye that doesn't see the eyelash says it will give the command.
A person who does not see the obvious but who wants to be in charge.

Chik pa respekte mèt bitasyon.
The flea has no respect for the plantation owner.
Troubles come to the wealthy as well as to the poor.

Kaka poul pa ze.
Chicken droppings are not eggs.
The same person is capable of both good and bad.

Ti pwason swiv kouran.
The little fish follows the current.
The little man follows the crowd.

Mèt kay manje panno kay.
The master of the house eats the walls.
He is in charge and will do as he pleases.

Bò tèt joumou an se pou mèt kay la.
The top of the pumpkin is for the master of the house.
Those in charge receive the best. Rank has its privileges.

Gran ke wa yo ye, yo menm bagay ak nou.
As great as the kings are, they are just like us.
Inside, we are all human.

Zandolit pa mete kanson mabouya.
A chameleon doesn't put on an iguana's pants.
A little man should not pretend to be a big shot.

Malere toujou bouke; gran nèg toujou nan vakans.
The poor man is always tired; the big shot is always on vacation.
The poor must work while the rich enjoy life.

Abitan pa mize lavil.
A peasant doesn't doddle downtown.
One doesn't spend time in an unfamiliar environment.

Sèvyèt tounen tòchon, tòchon tounen sèvièt.
The napkin turns into a dishrag; the dishrag turns into a napkin.
The rich become poor, the poor become rich.

Pitit malere maledve; pitit gran nèg malapri.
The poor man's child is ill bred; the rich man's child learned poorly.
Those with money are assumed to be better than those without.

Ti chwal kouri ak ti chwal, gwo chwal kouri ak gwo chwal.
The little horse runs with the little horse; the big horse runs with the big horse.
People stick with their own.

Jako nan mòn pa kondwi jako lavil.
The mountain parrot doesn't direct the town parrot.
A city person knows more than a country peasant.

Bèf pou wa, savann pou wa.
The pasture of the king's cow is for the king.
The representative of an important person does what he wants to.

Pye pay feye pou rasin li.
The palm tree leafs out for its roots.
Taking care of your own.

Sa malere di pa gen valè, betiz gran nèg se bon pawòl.
What the poor say has no value; the nonsense of the wealthy
is wisdom.
Money brings one respect.

Malere pa janm gen rezon devan gran nèg.
The poor man is never right before the big shot.
The rich and powerful are always seen as right.

Matla te di plis pase sa, epi li kite payas monte l'.
The mattress said the most, and then he let the straw mat
get the best of him.
The stronger man let himself be bested by a weaker one.

Malere vòlè; gran nèg pèdi lajan.
The poor rob, the wealthy lose money.
Description is a matter of perspective.

Lè ou pran sadin, li conprann se vyann li ye.
When you take the sardine, he thinks he's real meat.
When you help little people they think they are important.

Rat manje kann fè zandolit mouri inosan.
The rat eats the sugar cane and makes the innocent lizard
die.
The innocent poor reap the consequences of others' crimes.

Pise tig pa byè.
Tiger piss is not beer.
He is powerful but don't worship him. He is still human.

Ravèt pa janm gen rezon devan poul.
The cockroach is never right before a chicken.
The weak are powerless before the strong.

De towo pa rete nan menm savann.
Two bulls don't stay in the same pasture.
A situation can't have two chiefs (leaders).

Lavalas swen kouran.
The torrent cares for the creek.
A popular leader must care for his followers.

Ougan pa janm geri maleng li.
The witchdoctor never heals his own sores.
Even the powerful need help.

Nanpwen towo pase towo.
There's no more bull than a bull.
All leaders are equally bad.

Chen fè l', kochon ba l' tete.
A dog gave him birth, and a pig suckled him.
He's a low-life.

Van pran pilon; se pa laye li pa ta pran.
The wind carries away the mortar and pestle; it's not the
winnowing tray that it wouldn't take.
If the leader falls his followers will fall. Harm comes to all.

Baton ki bat chen blanch la, se li ki va bat chen nwa a.
The stick that beats the white dog will beat the black dog,
too.
*When misfortune strikes, nobody is immune. Your turn will
come.*

Twò rich pa mal; se tounen pòv ki pi rèd.
Too rich isn't bad; it's returning to poverty that's tough.
*A taste of the good life makes one sorry to return to a lesser
state.*

Lè vant chat plen, li di ke rat anmè.
When the cat is full, it says the rat's tail is bitter.
One is choosier when not in need.

Sa ki pa bon pou makout, li pa bon pou ralfò nonplis.
What's not good for the big sack, it's not good for the little sack either.
Don't give to the poor what you wouldn't want for yourself.

Ou menm ak kokobe kouche nan menm kabann.
You and the crippled sleep in the same bed.
A person who is underperforming.

Twòp lajan fè yon nonm pèdi tèt li.
Too much money makes a man lose his head.
Money makes one loose sight of priorities.

Lè de gran nèg ap regle zafè yo, piti, rale kò ou.
When two big shots are settling their affairs, little one, pull back.
Power colliding with power brings danger to others.

Pye nan chemen, chouk nan gran chemen.
Tree in the path, stump in the road.
A person who was important in a little situation but who cannot handle a larger situation.

Lè ou malere tout bagay sanble ou.
When you are poor, everything looks like you.
When you are poor, people will offer anything to you.

Lè nèg razè se lè a li pi bwòdè.
When a guy is flat broke is when he is cockiest.
The rich don't need to put on airs.

Gonfleman rich vanje grangou pòv.
The indigestion of the rich avenges the hunger of the poor.
People are amused at the problems greed brings to others.

Ti nèg fè sa l' kapab. Gran nèg fè sa l' vle.
The little guy does what he can. The big shot does what he
wants.
Those without power don't have the luxury of choice.

Se lè boutèy fin plen, bouchon jwen.
It is when the bottle is filled that the cork gets any.
The little man receives his share after the big shot is satisfied.

Ou wè mare chwal; mare bourik.
You see the marshal; tie your donkey.
*The police are around; do things right. (This proverb is a triple
play on Creole words. A marshal (marechal) is often jokingly
called a "mare chwal," which means to "tie up your horse." This
nickname comes from the fact that one of the responsibilities
a marechal has is to gather up stray animals that wander into
other people's gardens and make the owners pay a fine to get
them back.)*

Lè ou kontre zo nan granchemen, sonje se vyann ki te
kouvri li.
When you discover a bone on the highway, remember that
flesh once covered it.
Everyone was somebody once.

WALLY R. TURNBULL

TRANSLATOR, INTERPRETER, PHOTOGRAPHER

Wally Turnbull was born and raised in Haiti where he resided until 1963 when he left to pursue his education in the U.S.A.

Turnbull received his BA in Psychology from Rockford University in 1970 and his MFA from Ohio University in 1972.

He returned to Haiti with his wife Betty in 1972 where the couple worked until 2003 in rural education and self-help development with the Baptist Haiti Mission. The couple has three children, all of whom were born and raised in Haiti.

In 1978, Turnbull received a Diplôme de Citation from the Haitian Department of Education for his work in rural education. He also received an award of distinction from Rockford College in 1983 for his humanitarian work in Haiti.

Turnbull is the author of *Creole Made Easy*, and his photography is featured in *God is No Stranger*, a collection of Haitian prayers.

Si Bondye voye ou, li peye frè ou.

If God sends you, He pays your expenses.

God will take care of you if you do His will.

www.creolemadeeasy.com

**Nou pa mande pitit samble papa l',
nou mande erèz kouch.**

We don't ask for the baby to look like his father;
we just ask for a happy delivery.

*May the project be successful,
even if it turns out differently than anticipated.*

Figi ou se paspò ou.

Your face is your passport.

A good reputation will take you anywhere.

Timoun pa chen, granmoun pa Bondyè.

Children aren't dogs, adults aren't God.

Treat others with respect, and remember that nobody is perfect.